MARY CHENEY

Now It's My Turn

A Daughter's Chronicle of Political Life

THRESHOLD
EDITIONS

New York   London   Toronto   Sydney

THRESHOLD EDITIONS
Rockefeller Center
1230 Avenue of the Americas
New York, NY 10020

Threshold Editions and colophon are trademarks of
Simon & Schuster, Inc.

Designed by Jan Pisciotta

Manufactured in the United States of America

10   9   8   7   6   5   4   3   2   1

Library of Congress Cataloging-in-Publication Data

Cheney, Mary.
    Now it's my turn : a daughter's chronicle of political life / Mary Cheney.
        p.   cm.
    ISBN-13: 978-1-4165-2290-4
    ISBN-10:   1-4165-2290-5
    1. Cheney, Mary.   2. Cheney, Richard B.—Family.   3. Cheney, Richard B.
4. Daughters—United States—Biography.   5. Vice-Presidents—United States—
Biography.   6. Presidents—United States—Election—2000.   7. Presidents—
United States—Election—2004.   8. United States—Politics and government—
1993–2001.   9. United States—Politics and government—2001–   I. Title.

E840.8.C43C48   2006
973.931092—dc22   2006040453

For information regarding special discounts for bulk purchases,
please contact Simon & Schuster Special Sales at 1-800-456-6798 or
business@simonandschuster.com.

To my mother and father

Acknowledgments

I want to thank my parents and my sister, Liz, who helped me remember the experiences we've shared and offered a constant stream of support and encouragement. My favorite memories of writing this book are of the four of us sitting around the table, reminiscing about all of our campaigns together.

Much gratitude to my lawyer, Bob Barnett, who helped guide me through the world of publishing, who always gives me great advice, and who never stopped advocating on behalf of this book.

To Mary Matalin, who started the Threshold imprint, my thanks for being a trusted friend and advisor and for all of the backyard barbecues that helped shape this book. If anyone deserves the title of honorary member of the Cheney family, it's you.

To my editor, Ruth Fecych, my thanks for the suggestions and questions that helped make this a better book. To Jack Romanos, Carolyn Reidy, David Rosenthal, Louise Burke, and the rest of the Simon & Schuster team, my gratitude for all your hard work and support.

To David Bohrer, David Kennerly, and Mike Green, my deep appreciation for the work you do. Your photographs, some of which are included in this book, have preserved amazing moments in my life and in the life of the country.

To Kara Ahern, Taylor Talt, Steve Schmidt, Ben Ginsberg, Maria Cino, Elizabeth Kleppe, Ted Olson, Ron Walker, Pete Piraino, Jim Steen, Liz Denny, Ashley Snee, and Marguerite Sullivan, my thanks

ACKNOWLEDGMENTS

for taking the time to answer my questions and to share your campaign insights and stories.

To Debbie Heiden, Jen Field, Scooter Libby, Elizabeth Mason, Stephanie Lundberg, Jenny Mayfield, John McConnell, Brian McCormack, Neil Patel, Sarah Straka, Dan Wilmot, Anne Womack, and everyone else at the Bush-Cheney '04 campaign, the Republican National Committee, and the White House, your tireless work helped ensure victory, and I'm proud to have been on your team.

Lastly, to my incredible partner, Heather: Without your love and support, none of this would have been possible.

Contents

Now
It's
My Turn

CHAPTER 1

The Decision

Early in the summer of 2000, Dad invited me to go with him on a trip to South America. We spent a week sitting in duck blinds in Argentina, hunting perdiz in Uruguay, and talking about typical father-daughter topics: my plans for starting business school in the fall, how the rest of the family was doing, and whether or not we would be able to get in a few days of fishing in Jackson Hole later that summer.

It wasn't until we were halfway into the flight home that he turned to me and asked, "What do you think about me running for vice president?" The question caught me so off-guard that at first I thought he was kidding. After all, my dad had given every indication that he was done with politics. He and my mom were happily living in Dallas, Texas, where he was the CEO of Halliburton, a Fortune 500 company, and he was doing the kinds of things that former politicians do, like helping Governor George W. Bush, the presumptive Republican nominee for president, find a running mate. Besides, at first glance, my dad seemed like an odd choice for vice president. It had been twelve years since he last ran for office, and while he led an active and vigorous life, he had a history of heart disease. In addition, he was from Wyoming, a state with three of the safest, most dependable, most Republican electoral votes in the country. Nominating Dick Cheney to be vice president violated just about every piece of conventional political wisdom I could think of.

Once the initial shock wore off, however, I realized that he wasn't joking. He was doing what he does so often, bringing up a subject he'd given a lot of thought to—but that no one else would have guessed he was pondering. I'd spent the last week with him and didn't have a clue.

My dad told me that Joe Allbaugh, Governor Bush's campaign manager, had come to see him in March about the possibility of his being the running mate. Dad told Joe that he was happy in private life. His political career was over, and besides, he didn't think it made political sense for him to be the vice presidential nominee. He recommended that the campaign consider other candidates. Later, when Governor Bush called and asked him to head up a search committee for a running mate, he agreed to help out.

Dad had spent the spring of 2000 working on the vice presidential search effort with a small team of advisors. He had also gotten better acquainted with George W. Bush, his character and his ideas. He was impressed with everything the governor had accomplished during his time in Austin and with his plans for the presidency. From the beginning, Governor Bush had made it clear that he wasn't just looking for a running mate who could help him get elected. He wanted a running mate who could help him govern. From time to time he also made it clear that he still wanted my dad to be on the list of possible candidates, and in a phone call right before Dad had left on our hunting trip, Governor Bush had made the point again, forcefully. With his experience in Congress, as

White House chief of staff and secretary of defense, it would be difficult to find someone more qualified to help govern than my dad.

Everyone expected Governor Bush to make his decision before the start of the Republican National Convention at the end of July. Now it was the first of July, and my dad was asking what I thought about the idea of his joining the ticket.

We spent the rest of the flight home from South America talking about what a run for national office would mean for our family, particularly for me. A national campaign would subject everyone in our family to intense media scrutiny, and he was concerned that people would target me and my sexual orientation in an attempt to attack him. He wanted to make sure I understood exactly what this decision could mean.

"Personally," I told him, "I'd rather not be known as the vice president's lesbian daughter. But, if you're going to run, I think the country would be lucky to have you. I want to do whatever I can to help out on the campaign. And you'd better win."

Dad explained that it was far from a done deal. The governor had indicated that he wanted to consider him, but Dad hadn't yet agreed. And there was still a very real possibility that the governor would choose someone else. As head of the search committee, my dad's job was to make sure that Governor Bush had all of the information he needed to make that decision.

Over the next few days we had several family discussions about the possibility of Dad's running for vice president. My mom was the least enthusiastic about the idea. Life as we all knew it was good, she said. Why take a leap into the great unknown? And what would it mean for her career? Could she continue to sit on any of the corporate boards she was on? Could she keep writing? My sister, Liz, was wholeheartedly in favor of his running. We joked that she had already started painting "Cheney for Veep" campaign signs in her backyard. I was somewhere in the middle. I thought Dad would be an excellent vice president and that it would be exciting to be part of a national campaign, but there was no doubt that it would change my life—and I was very happy with the way it was: living quietly in the mountains of Colorado and looking forward to starting business school in the fall.

I also had to consider Heather Poe, my partner, and her feelings on the matter. She is a smart, warm, funny, and incredibly private person who rarely enjoys being at the center of attention. Heather and I first met when I was in college—I was on the women's hockey team and Heather played for one of the other teams in the league, and we started dating about a year after I graduated. In the eight years that we had been together, we had pretty successfully managed to stay out of the spotlight, but that was likely to change if Dad became the vice presidential nominee. We had several long discussions about what it would be like: reporters calling, even staking out the house; political extremists protesting in our neighborhood. We'd lose the anonymity that allowed us to go to the grocery store or snowboarding or whatever we wanted to do without people watching our every move—and reporting it to the gossip columns. Heather was not thrilled with the idea of herself and our private life being pushed into the public eye, but she is calm, steady, and generous of spirit. "It's not my first choice," she said, "but I love you and we'll figure out a way to deal with whatever happens next."

While the rest of the family was busy debating whether we thought Dad should run, he continued trying to find the best possible vice presidential candidate for Governor Bush. On July 3, two days after we returned from South America, Dad flew down to the governor's ranch in Crawford, Texas, for the last major review of potential running mates.

After they'd gone through the list of candidates, Governor Bush invited my dad out to the back porch of the ranch house. Sitting out there, in the stifling Texas summer heat, Governor Bush said,

"You know, Dick, you're the solution to my problem." Dad agreed to explore what he would have to do in order to be a viable candidate. One crucial step, because of his history of heart disease, was to get a medical checkup. He flew to Washington, D.C., had a stress test, and put his cardiologist in touch with the well-known Texas heart surgeon Denton Cooley. A few days later, my parents were in Minnesota, where my mom was attending a board meeting, when Dad was called out of a dinner to take a call from Governor Bush. The governor told him that he had talked to Denton Cooley, who said there was no medical reason that would prohibit my dad from running for vice president. This was great news, of course, but my dad said that he wanted to be very sure that the governor had fully considered the downside of choosing him. He wanted the opportunity to lay out the case against himself as the nominee.

The next weekend, Dad flew to Austin to meet with Governor Bush, Karen Hughes, and Karl Rove. Dad spoke in very direct terms about his health, saying that if he experienced chest pain, he had to go to the hospital immediately and that this was not likely to have positive political benefits during a presidential campaign. He also spoke about his conservative voting record and the fact that he and the governor were both residents of Texas and had been involved in the oil business. Knowing my dad, I'm sure he didn't hold anything back as he laid out the disadvantages of selecting him as the nominee. He can be totally candid, even when it's not in his own interest to do so, a trait that makes him pretty unusual in politics.

The meeting ended with no decision. At that point, there was still one other candidate under serious consideration—John Danforth of Missouri, a well-respected senator from a key battleground state. In mid-July, my dad arranged for Senator Danforth and his wife to meet with the governor in Chicago. He accompanied the Danforths to the Hyatt Hotel off Michigan Avenue, where

Governor Bush was staying, then left the three of them while they discussed the senator's possible candidacy.

But as time went on, it looked increasingly as though Dad was going to be the governor's choice. There remained, however, one major obstacle to his joining the ticket: his Texas residency. According to the Twelfth Amendment, a state's electors are prohibited from casting their votes for both a presidential and a vice presidential candidate from that same state. If my dad was going to be the nominee, he would have to reestablish his residency in Wyoming, where he had grown up, lived for over forty years, and been the congressman for a decade, or he would risk losing the Texas electoral votes. On July 21, the last possible day to register to vote in the Wyoming primary, he flew from Dallas to Jackson, Wyoming, where he and my mom had a home, and registered to vote. Then he dropped by the Motor Vehicles Department and obtained a Wyoming driver's license.

These activities did not go unnoticed. It wasn't long before all of the networks and wire services speculated that Dad would be on the ticket. My sister, Liz, was getting her hair cut at a salon in Georgetown when she received an urgent call from the campaign. Dad hadn't told anyone there what he was going to do, so they were trying to understand the news reports. "Liz, you're a lawyer," Joe Allbaugh said, "so maybe you can explain to me exactly what your dad is doing in Wyoming." Liz, her hair dripping wet, didn't want anyone in the salon to overhear the conversation, so she shut herself into a utility closet and walked Joe Allbaugh through the intricacies of the Twelfth Amendment.

By the time Dad landed in Washington, the media had set up a stakeout across the street from the McLean, Virginia, townhouse, where my parents stayed when they were in Washington. With the press ready to pounce, it was hard for them to go outside, and even inside wasn't entirely safe. At one point, the doorbell rang. My mom was coming down the stairs to answer it, when she saw Sam Donaldson standing on the front porch staring in the window. He spotted my mom and started yelling, "Lynne! Lynne! It's Sam!" Mom changed her mind about answering the door. She ducked back out of sight as quickly as she could.

After being under siege by the press corps for a day or so, Dad decided that he had to get out of the house, if only to visit the local bookstore. He and my brother-in-law, Phil, devised a plan that was quickly dubbed "The Great Escape." Phil would park his car down at the end of the street and wait. Dad and Liz would go to the garage. Dad would get into the car, turn it on, and signal Liz to open the garage door. He would then drive off while Phil blocked the road with his car to keep the press from following. During the planning process, my mom kept saying, "This is not a good idea." Her prediction would prove to be correct.

Everything went as planned until Dad signaled Liz to open the garage door. She pushed the button and he gunned the car into reverse. Unfortunately, he didn't wait for the door to open quite far enough and he backed into the garage door, denting the car and knocking the door off its tracks.

From their vantage point across the street, the press captured the entire incident on tape, and several of the cable networks ran it regularly throughout the day. Dad never did make it to the bookstore. Instead, he, my mom, and Liz returned to Dallas to wait for Governor Bush's decision. I was at home in Colorado. I would have loved to have been with my parents, but if my dad was the nominee, I was going to be working on the campaign. I didn't know exactly what my job would be, but I knew that it would keep me on the road until Election Day, and I needed to prepare. I had to change my plans about business school, buy some dark suits, a staple of campaign life, but not something people tend to wear very often in the mountains of Colorado, and I needed to pack.

My dad was working out on the treadmill when Governor Bush called and officially asked him to be his running mate. Dad agreed to join the ticket and made arrangements to travel down to Austin for the official announcement.

Governor Bush introduced my dad as his running mate at a rally at the University of Texas on July 25. He said he chose my dad not because of Wyoming's three electoral votes, but because my dad was "fully capable of being president."

Vice presidential nominees are usually chosen because they are from a key state or region, they have a large constituency within the party, or they've been a runner-up for the presidential nomination. As far as I know, this was the first time a running mate had been chosen for the qualities he could bring to the responsibilities of governing, rather than because of some geographic or demographic appeal he could bring to the ticket. Some of the talking heads on television said that the selection of my dad showed that Governor Bush was so confident of winning that he wasn't worried about trying to broaden his appeal. What it really showed was how seriously he took the job of president of the United States. He was more concerned with selecting someone who could help him govern than he was with choosing the most politically advantageous running mate.

As Heather and I watched the announcement on the television in our living room, our phone started ringing and we found ourselves inundated by calls from reporters and producers who wanted to interview the gay daughter of the Republican vice presidential nominee.

There were well over a hundred calls in the first twenty-four hours, all of which we let the answering machine pick up. As amazing as the volume of calls was the fact that everyone left work and home phone numbers. It wasn't just the producers. Maria Shriver,

Diane Sawyer, and Connie Chung all left their home phone numbers, but Heather and I didn't return any of the calls. These reporters only wanted to talk to me about my sexual orientation, and they only wanted to talk to me about that because my dad was a candidate for vice president. I had better things to do. Heather and I did write down everyone's name and number, however. We toyed with the idea of auctioning off the list on eBay, but decided that it probably wasn't a good idea to alienate all of those reporters at the start of a national political campaign.

Without a doubt, the most persistent reporter was Diane Sawyer. She called, or had someone call on her behalf, five separate times. Because we were so impressed by this level of determination, we saved those messages.

Message 1
"Hi, Mary. This is Mark Robertson calling from Diane Sawyer's office. Diane would really like to talk to you. Please call me back at xxx-xxx-xxxx, and I'll connect you."

Message 2
"Mary, it's Mark Robertson again from Diane Sawyer's office. Hope you don't mind, but I gave your number to Diane. She really wants to talk to you and just see how you're doing with everything. You can reach me at xxx-xxx-xxxx. Talk to you soon."

Message 3
"Mary Cheney. This is Diane Sawyer. I've known your parents for years and can't imagine everything you and your family are going through right now, but would love to talk to you and see how you're holding up. Hope you saw the piece I did on Ellen. Please call me—xxx-xxx-xxxx."

Message 4

"Mary, hi, this is pesky Mark Robertson again in Diane Sawyer's office. I'm so sorry to bug you but was watching the *Today* show this morning and they sort of put all of this into play by saying, you know, Dick Cheney's openly gay daughter, which we all cheered for, but I just wanted you to know if you ever want to see the piece Diane did on Ellen or the thing she won a GLAAD award for this year on Billy Bean the professional baseball player who had to deal with this publicly, I'd love to send them to you, and Diane was wanting to talk to you. I think she called and left you a message and she's at home today and I wanted to leave you her home phone number, which is xxx-xxx-xxxx. I know she just wants to say hello and somebody else, Ellen, has asked me for your phone number 'cause she's friends of mine and Diane's and she's heard about this and just wanted to wish you well I think, so if it's OK just if you'd call me at xxx-xxx-xxxx, I'll give her that number and if not, I won't. So thanks so much. Bye."

Message 5

"Well hello, Mary, this is someone you don't know. It's Ellen DeGeneres and I just spoke with Mark, Diane Sawyer's producer, and they tell me you're going through a lot of stuff, so I thought I'd call and see if I can be of any help at all. Just support, I guess, and so call me if you'd like to. It's xxx-xxx-xxxx and we'll talk, all right? Bye."

The only person I was tempted to call back was Ellen DeGeneres. I was a fan, and I appreciated her willingness to call a perfect stranger to offer her support, but mostly I was curious to find out what stuff Mark Robertson had told her I was going through. As far as I was concerned, my only problem was that the media wouldn't stop calling.

To escape the onslaught, I drove to Casper, Wyoming, where my parents and the Bushes were scheduled to hold a rally at Natrona County High School, my parents' alma mater. I knew there would be press at the rally, but figured that at least no one could reach me during the drive up and back.

Up until this time I'd been so busy worrying about whether or not my dad was going to be the nominee, packing for life on the road, and postponing business school that the magnitude of what we were doing hadn't really had a chance to sink in. It wasn't until I watched my parents walk down the stairs of the campaign plane with the governor and Mrs. Bush that it hit me. We were jumping off a cliff. At least that's what it felt like. I just hoped that the landing would be soft.

I hugged my parents and was introduced to the Bushes, whom I had never met, and before I could ask where I was supposed to go, an efficient young staffer carrying a notebook and wearing a radio grabbed me by the arm and politely, but firmly, escorted me to a van in the motorcade.

The motorcade for a presidential nominee is an impressive sight: a long line of dark cars, flashing lights, sirens, Secret Service agents, and enough weapons to start, or stop, a small war. Police officers on motorcycles halt traffic at all intersections so that the motorcade never has to stop, or even slow down, at a red light or a stop sign. The principals, in this case my parents and the Bushes, ride near the front and are driven by Secret Service agents. All others—staff, guests, and members of the press—ride in cars driven by local volunteers. Each driver is instructed to stay right on the bumper of the car in front of him. Drivers near the front of the motorcade are used to traveling at high speeds in close formation, but if you are in one of the cars near the back of the motorcade, it can be a bit of an adventure. I was in the back of the motorcade.

It took a few minutes for me to accept the fact that maintaining a death grip on the back of the driver's seat wasn't going to keep our car from slamming into the car in front of us, but I finally managed to sit back and enjoy the ride. I just had to avoid looking out the front windshield, a strategy I still use whenever I ride in a motorcade.

The city of Casper gave my parents an incredible homecoming. People lined the streets holding up hand-painted signs that said "Wyoming's Own," "Welcome Home Dick and Lynne," and "Wyoming is Cheney Country." My favorites were the people holding up blue and white "Cheney for Congress" signs left over from my dad's congressional campaigns.

At the high school gym, the crowd was enthusiastic, energetic, and filled with friends and relatives. So many people showed up for the rally that the crowd overflowed into another room. In order to thank everyone, Dad and Governor Bush gave their speeches in the gym and worked the ropeline, then repeated it all in the overflow room.

During the visit to the overflow room, I was standing off to the side with Liz when Howard Fineman from *Newsweek* came up and introduced himself. He was polite, but had obviously zeroed in on me. He started peppering me with questions: How did I feel about Dad joining the ticket; what was I going to be doing on the campaign; how did I feel about all of the attention that the media was paying to my sexual orientation; was I worried that the fact that I was gay was going to be an issue in the campaign?

I decided that the best course of action was simply to ignore him. By then the rally was over, so Liz and I followed our parents into the school's band room, where Dad and Governor Bush were about to do an interview. The interview was with Howard Fineman.

The three of them were in one of the practice rooms off to the side. It had glass walls, so we could see them, but it was soundproofed, so we couldn't hear what was said. Seeing was enough.

Someone had apparently told Dad about Fineman's interrogating me minutes earlier. Dad may not be the most animated person, but it's pretty easy to tell when he's mad, and he was mad. I'm not sure exactly what he said to Howard Fineman, but whatever it was, it worked. It's been almost six years since that rally in Casper—and since Howard Fineman last spoke to me.

I rode back to the airport with my parents and watched their plane take off. My plan was to take a couple more days to wrap things up at home, meet them in Washington, and then fly to Philadelphia with them for the convention.

As I drove home to Colorado, I thought about everything that had happened in the last few days and everything that lay ahead. I'd never worked in a national campaign, but I knew that this was going to be the World Series, the Stanley Cup, the Triple Crown of political experiences. I was pretty sure that there were going to be days I'd hate, but it was impossible not to be excited about being part of something as big as electing a president and vice president of the United States.

CHAPTER 2

Growing Up in Politics

My first political memory is a sweet one—a chocolate, peanut butter and jelly one, to be exact. I was five years old, my dad was deputy assistant to the president, working for Don Rumsfeld, who was then President Ford's chief of staff, and every Saturday morning, Dad would take me and my sister, Liz, with him to the White House. Our first activity was always the same—raiding the stash of candy outside Don Rumsfeld's office. His secretary, Brenda Williams, kept a desk drawer full of all sorts of miniature candy bars, and since she always let us choose a couple of pieces when she was there, we figured it was probably OK for us to choose a couple when she wasn't there as well. Just as impressive as the stockpile of candy was the jar of peanut butter and jelly that was in the desk. Liz and I were convinced that it was one of the greatest inventions of all time. We would stand there eating candy and trying to figure out how someone had managed to get perfect vertical columns of peanut butter and jelly into the same jar without mixing them together. It was truly amazing.

In November 1975, Don Rumsfeld became secretary of defense, and my dad took his place as White House chief of staff. I could tell that Dad was happy about his new job, but I wasn't completely thrilled, since I figured that the drawer of candy and the jar of peanut butter and jelly were going to be leaving along with Mr. Rumsfeld. It was my first experience with the emotional highs and lows and compromises that are part of a life in politics.

Growing up, people would periodically ask me what it was like to have parents who were involved in politics. It was a tough question to answer, since I didn't really have anything to compare it to. My parents moved to Washington, D.C., a few months before I was born so that my dad, then a graduate student at the University of Wisconsin, could accept a fellowship to study the Congress. With the exception of about ten months between the time President Ford left office and the time my dad decided to run for the House of Representatives from Wyoming, my parents were always involved in politics. As a kid, I just assumed that everyone walked door to door asking for votes, passed out campaign buttons, and worried about what was going to happen on the first Tuesday in November.

The first election night I remember worrying about was in 1976, the year Jimmy Carter ran against Gerald Ford. I was too young to understand all the details, but I knew that Gerald Ford was a good man and that we wanted him to win. As White House chief of staff, my dad oversaw Ford's campaign, which was tough going from day one. President Ford's pardoning of Richard Nixon after Watergate, although the right thing to do, hadn't been popular, and he faced a strong primary challenge from former California governor Ronald Reagan. At the start of the fall campaign, President Ford was trailing Governor Carter by almost thirty points in the polls, but he managed to fight back, and by Election Day, he had pulled to within striking distance.

On election night, my parents watched the returns at the White House, leaving Liz and me at home with a babysitter. She was an older woman who chain-smoked and had some rather strong opinions. At one point during the evening, she picked up a copy of *Time* magazine, and, with her lit cigarette, burned out the eyes in the cover photo of Idi Amin. It was the kind of thing that made a big impression on a seven-year-old. Looking back on it now, it's the kind of thing that makes me wonder where our parents found our babysitters.

Ultimately, President Ford came up just short of victory, but it took all night for the final results to be confirmed. The next morning, when it was clear that it was over, President Ford, who had lost his voice in the last days of the campaign, asked my dad to help him out with the concession call to Jimmy Carter. President Ford was able to squeeze out a few words on the phone, then he turned the call over to my dad, who read a prepared statement congratulating the governor on his victory. It's the only time Dad has ever had to concede an election.

On January 20, 1977, after President Carter's inauguration, my mom drove my sister and me to Andrews Air Force Base, where President Ford was leaving to go back to California. As soon as the plane took off, all the Ford men who had been wearing radios and earpieces tossed them into an aluminum suitcase that someone had brought out onto the tarmac. Dad joined us in the family station wagon and we went across the street to a McDonald's for lunch. At the time it seemed like the most normal thing in the world. As I think back on it now, it also seems very American. One minute you're helping run the free world, and the next minute, you're at McDonald's—and out of work.

My parents decided to go back home to Wyoming, so Mom took care of getting our house cleaned out and sold, and my dad made two trips to Casper driving U-Haul trucks full of all our belongings. On the second trip, he towed our 1965 black Volkswagen Bug, and I went along for the ride. My mom had packed our house plants into the VW, and, worrying that I might grow lazy and bored on the two-thousand-mile drive, she assigned me a task. Every time we gassed up, I had to open the Volkswagen and spray the plants with water from an old Windex bottle.

A few months after we moved home, Teno Roncalio, Wyoming's sole congressman, announced he would not be seeking re-election in 1978, and it didn't take Dad long to declare for his seat. He'd gone back to Wyoming with the idea that he'd run for office from there someday, and though he hadn't expected an opening so soon, he knew that you have to take your opportunities when they come, so we were back in politics. My father's first run for public office was about as far as you could get from a presidential campaign. The whole family, including my grandparents, piled into a rented Winnebago, and with Grandpa driving, we traveled all over the state. There weren't a lot of radio stations to choose from, so we usually ended up listening to my dad's rather impressive collection of eight-track tapes, which seemed to include just about every song ever performed by the Carpenters.

Grandma would keep an eye on me and Liz. My mom was chief political advisor and Liz was in charge of passing out "Cheney for Congress" campaign buttons. As the youngest member of the family, I was assigned to a series of odd jobs: throwing candy whenever we rode in a parade, accompanying my parents when they walked door to door, and, the assignment I'm proudest of, standing on the corner outside campaign headquarters wearing a sandwich board that said "Honk for Cheney."

Even though we were young, Liz and I never passed up an opportunity to win one more vote for our dad. Whenever we hit a construction delay on the highway, we'd jump out of the Winnebago and hand out campaign buttons and bumper stickers to all the cars waiting for the highway crew to let them pass. After working one particularly long stretch of cars, we climbed back into the RV, thirsty and dusty, but quite proud of all the buttons we'd passed out. Then Grandpa turned around in the driver's seat and asked the crucial question: "Girls, how many of those cars have Wyoming plates?" Given that it was a busy interstate in the middle of summer, the answer was not many.

Campaigning in Wyoming is politics at its most retail level. It's done one voter at a time. If we had more than ten people show up for a single event, it was a huge deal. My dad once drove three hours from Casper to Laramie to have coffee with three voters, two of whom had been in my parents' wedding. The best way to work a town was to walk down its main street with someone local who could introduce you to all the shop owners or take you to the coffee shop—the Cozy Cup in Riverton was a great one—where you could hear what was on people's minds. There were a few towns where my parents didn't know anyone, but in Wyoming, nobody is more than one or two steps removed from anyone else. Someone's best friend would own the local farm implement store, or would have played high school football with the local Ford dealer. It just took some time to figure out what all the relationships were.

One of the best ways to meet local community leaders was to arrange an invitation to speak at one of the local service organizations like the Kiwanis or the Rotary. One gentleman introduced my dad at a local Lions Club by saying, "This is Dick Cheney. He says that he used to work in Washington, D.C., and that he was White House chief of staff. The guy who had the job before him was Don Rumsfeld. He ended up being secretary of defense. Before Rumsfeld it was Al Haig. He's our commander at NATO. The guy who had it before Al Haig is Bob Haldeman, who's doing five to ten in a federal penitentiary. Anyway, here he is." It was less than a rousing endorsement, but at least it allowed my dad to get his foot in the door.

In 1978, there was only one television station in Wyoming, KTWO in Casper, which meant that local radio was crucial. Whenever Dad was going to a town, he'd call up the local station and try to set up an interview or at least arrange to drop by so he could meet the station manager. One morning, doing one of his drop-bys in Evanston, he found the station empty. Music was playing on the turntable, and he noticed that flies were buzzing around one of the trash cans, but there wasn't a person in sight. Then a guy walked in the back door of the station wearing bloodstained bib overalls, no shirt, and carrying a big, bloody butcher knife. He was the station DJ who was supposed to interview my dad, but earlier that morning, he'd shot a deer out behind the radio station, and now he was in the middle of butchering it. He was perfectly friendly, but told Dad that he was just too busy cleaning his deer to talk to some guy who was running for Congress.

Another downside to local radio was that sometimes it didn't seem that many people tuned in. I remember driving with my mom while we listened to my dad on a call-in show in Lander in the middle of the afternoon. The interviewer kept giving the phone number and inviting people to call with their questions, but no one did. Finally, it was too much for my mom. She found a pay phone, dug a quarter out of her purse, and called in to the show so it would sound like there was at least some interest in my dad's candidacy. Fortunately, the only person who recognized her voice was Dad. He didn't let on that he knew it was she, but when he got home, he suggested that it might be a good idea for her not to do that again.

What I loved most about that first campaign were the parades. Just about every town in Wyoming has an annual parade, often in connection with the local rodeo. Participants include everyone

from candidates running for office to the local Little League baseball teams to the omnipresent Shriners wearing fezzes and driving
their minicars and bikes. Given the size of some of the towns, it
wasn't unusual to have more people marching and riding in the parade than watching it.

One of my favorite parades was in Thermopolis. The whole parade marched up one side of a divided street, made a U-turn, and
went back down the other side of the same street. In most parades,
I rarely got to see anything but the car we were riding in and the
cars ahead of us and behind us, but in Thermopolis I got to see the
whole parade as it marched down the street in the other direction.

Each member of the Cheney family had an assigned parade
task. My parents would ride in a convertible, preferably an old clas-
sic car, smiling, waving, and shouting greetings to people they
knew. Liz would walk alongside the car and pass out "Cheney for
Congress" buttons. I would sit in the backseat with my parents and
throw candy to the kids in the crowd. My parents gave me only two
instructions that I had to follow: (1) Make sure to throw the candy
far enough from the car so that no one got run over while trying to
retrieve a piece of bubble gum, and (2) pace myself. The candy
had to last for the whole parade. This was especially true in Thermopolis. If you gave out candy to people on one side of the divided
street, then ran out, everyone on the other side would know it.

Most parades were pretty easy. The only problem I remember
was in Douglas at the kickoff parade for the Wyoming State Fair. As
usual, my parents were waving, I was throwing candy, and Liz was
passing out buttons. Because it was the state fair, the crowds were
larger than usual, and Liz, who was determined to make sure that
everyone who wanted a button got one, had trouble keeping up
with the car. Pretty soon she had fallen so far behind that she was
bringing up the rear of the parade. That turned out to be a confus-
ing place to be, because as the parade passed, all the people who'd

been watching picked up their lawn chairs and headed toward the fairgrounds. As they all marched straight ahead, Liz couldn't see that the parade turned right, and she marched straight ahead, too. When we got to the end of the parade route, there was no sign of her, and a frantic search ensued. Personally, I wasn't quite as frantic as my parents were. I definitely wanted Liz to be OK, but I was kind of intrigued by the notion of being an only child, if even for just a short period of time. After scouring Douglas for twenty to thirty minutes, we found her sitting at the entrance to the fairgrounds drinking a Pepsi and holding her now empty white wicker basket. Even after she realized she was lost, she kept handing out "Cheney for Congress" buttons. That's dedication.

Our family had a lot of fun during that first campaign, traveling around the state together, with everyone pitching in to help get Dad elected. But one event was pretty traumatic. On a campaign trip to the southeastern part of the state, Dad had his first heart attack.

We had dropped Liz off in Laramie so she could spend a couple of days with friends, and I had gone on to Cheyenne with Mom and Dad. As we always did when we were in Cheyenne, we stayed with Joe and Mary Meyer, longtime friends of my parents. Joe and my dad had played football together at Natrona County High School. They'd been roommates at the University of Wyoming, and he'd been in my parents' wedding. Joe had even taken my mom out on a few dates when they were in high school.

The Meyers' son, Vince, was my age, and I was asleep on the floor of his room when my mom woke me up to tell me that she was taking my dad to the hospital. She told me not to worry, but, of course, I was still scared. Having something happen to your parents is one of the worst things any child can imagine. I'll never forget that feeling or that day, Sunday, June 18, 1978—Father's Day.

Dad woke up about two that morning with a tingling sensation in two of the fingers in his left hand. A couple of weeks earlier, one of his cousins, Gene Dickey, had suffered a very serious heart attack, so while my dad wasn't in pain, he decided to play it safe and have himself checked out.

Joe Meyer drove my parents to the hospital. Dad walked into the emergency room, sat down on the examining table, and passed out. It didn't take the doctors long to diagnose that, at the age of thirty-seven, he had had a heart attack. Part of the reason was genetic. His cousin wasn't the only male in his family to have coronary artery disease. Dad's grandfather had suffered from it as well, and we would later find out that his father (my grandfather) did, too. Grandpa didn't go to doctors much, but when he was in his seventies, he broke down and had a physical. His doctors discovered that he had had two heart attacks for which he'd never been treated.

But genes weren't the only factor. My dad is the first to admit that he spent a good portion of the 1970s living on caffeine and nicotine. At the time of his heart attack, he was smoking three packs of cigarettes a day. The doctors told him that he needed to give it up, start exercising regularly, and watch his diet. He quit smoking cold turkey, and he hasn't had a cigarette in the more than twenty-five years since. He also started exercising and got much better about eating right.

My dad's heart attack was mild, and none of the doctors suggested he pull out of the race. A doctor from Cheyenne, Rick Davis, gave him what seemed to be particularly good advice. "Hard work never hurt anybody," Davis said. "It's spending your life doing something you don't want to do that'll kill you."

My dad left the hospital determined to stay in the race, but he couldn't just jump right back into a full-speed congressional campaign. Under orders to take it easy for some weeks, he went home to Casper, sat under a big spruce tree in our backyard, and read

Richard Nixon's recently published memoirs. Mom filled in, doing some events on her own and making as many campaign decisions as she could without bothering my dad. My parents were also fortunate enough to have a big group of friends who helped out and offered encouragement. One of the first calls they got was from Foster Channock, an incredibly smart and funny man who had worked with my dad in the Ford White House. Foster wanted my folks to know that he was telling everyone to send campaign contributions, not flowers.

While he was recuperating, Dad sat down with Mom and several other advisors to figure out the politics of the situation. Bob Teeter, a trusted friend and a great pollster, came all the way from Michigan, and his conclusion was that there was no point in trying to poll on the matter. Nothing like this had ever happened before and he didn't think anyone could even figure out what questions to ask.

My parents shot a couple of television commercials that made the point that other public figures had had heart attacks and continued to serve. In one spot, they sat on our lawn and talked with a small group of people about Lyndon Johnson and Dwight Eisenhower. But the commercials never aired. Everybody agreed that they were too stark and unsettling. They just didn't work.

One thing my parents did do was send out a letter to every registered voter in the state in which my dad explained why he was staying in the race. He talked about how going through a crisis focuses you on what is important in life, how it makes you ask what you really want to spend your time doing. For him the answer was public service, and since the doctors had assured him there was no health reason for him to drop out, he intended to keep going—and to win.

By the end of July, he was ready to start campaigning again. He walked over to a gathering of senior citizens in a park near our house, made his way around to all the tables, and shook everyone's hand. We were back in business.

The primary was at the end of August and we knew it was going to be close. Dad was running against Ed Witzenberger, the state treasurer, and Jack Gage, whose father had been governor of the state during the 1960s. They both had great name recognition, and Barry Goldwater had made a trip to Wyoming to campaign for Ed Witzenberger. So, as the primary drew near, my parents took one of the biggest gambles of their lives. They took all the money they had, fifty thousand dollars that my mom's father had left them when he died, and put it into the campaign. They had to choose between spending the money on a poll to see where things stood or buying additional advertising. They decided on advertising, figuring that if they learned anything new from polling, they wouldn't have any money left to address it. It turned out to be the right call. Dad won the three-way primary with 41 percent of the vote and then went on to comfortably win the general election.

As I look back on that first campaign, I think how easy it would have been for Dad to have dropped out of the race, taken a low-pressure job somewhere, and spent the rest of his life worrying incessantly about his health. Instead, he confronted the problem, figured out how he was going to handle it, and then moved on. It's a pretty good model for how to get through a crisis—and how to live a life.

After that first campaign, Dad never had another close election, but he still took each of them seriously. He didn't want to be caught by surprise, or be seen by the people of Wyoming as taking an election for granted. While he never had another tough race, he did seem to have a knack for drawing some rather unique opponents.

There was the gentleman from Cheyenne (I'll call him Bill) who ran against my dad in the Republican primary. Bill's whole campaign was based on the position that people ought to have the right to grow their own marijuana. To make his point, he called the police to his house so he could show them his collection of marijuana plants. Understanding a public relations stunt when they saw one, the officers looked at the plants, thanked Bill for calling, and left without arresting him. Not easily dismissed, Bill then called the local newspaper and had them come out and take a picture of him with his favorite marijuana plant. This was too much for the local sheriff, who had him arrested and thrown into jail. What really amazed our whole family was that even after he was thrown into jail, Bill still received 10 percent of the vote in the Republican primary. We couldn't figure it out. Did that mean that 10 percent of the Republicans in Wyoming preferred pot-growing Bill to my dad? Did that mean that 10 percent of the voters had marked their ballots incorrectly and accidentally voted for Bill? Were 10 percent of the voters stoned? All of the explanations were a little disturbing, but the experience did reinforce the principle that no vote should ever be taken for granted.

There was the 1986 campaign where it looked like Dad might run unopposed. Wyoming has a two-week filing period for people who want to run for office, and by the final day of the filing period no one else had entered the race. At the last minute, a man I'll call Ron walked in and filed his papers to run for Congress. My dad didn't know who he was, but geared up for a full campaign anyway. He raised money, bought advertising, and even took part in a candidate's debate at the University of Wyoming. Ron, meanwhile, campaigned all over the state of Wyoming in a truck that had Idaho license plates. No one could figure out why he was running for Congress, and on Election Day, Dad beat him soundly. It wasn't until later that we learned that Ron had gotten into the race by mistake. Apparently, he had been at a bar with a bunch of his friends one night, and there'd been a debate about whether anyone in America could really run for office. Bets were placed, and the next day, Ron drove all the way to Cheyenne to file as a candidate for the state legislature. But he checked the wrong box on the form and unexpectedly found himself running for the U.S. House of Representatives. I don't know if Ron won his bet or not, but given that he campaigned all the way through to the election for an office he never intended to run for, he sure should have.

One story from Dad's congressional campaigns was his favorite, and he used it as the opening joke for just about every political speech he gave in Wyoming during the 1980s. He told it at his Senate confirmation hearing when he became secretary of defense. And it even appeared on the campaign trail once or twice during the 2000 and 2004 presidential campaigns. It's an absolutely true story, and it goes like this:

Early one morning during the 1980 campaign, Dad was scheduled to be on a call-in show on a radio station in Riverton, Wyoming. He'd spent the night before with some friends in Lander, just a few miles down the road, and he and his aide, Jack Berry, were driving over to Riverton, when they tuned in to the station to see what they were talking about. The host of the show was saying, "We don't know where Cheney is. He was supposed to be here ten minutes ago." Realizing that there must have been some sort of scheduling mix-up, Dad asked Jack to step on it.

Ten minutes later, Jack pulled into the gravel parking lot and parked near the building, where my dad had been many times before. It's on the south side of Riverton, just before you cross the Wind River, and there's a big sign on the building advertising the station's call letters. My dad jumped out of the car, took the stairs two at a time, threw open the station's front door, and ran inside. In his rush, he noticed what he thought was a person off to one side of the doorway, but didn't really focus on who it was. He made it all the way to the middle of the room before he realized that something wasn't right. It didn't look like a radio station. Through one door, he could see what looked like a kitchen and in the back there was a bedroom with a baby in diapers crawling around on the floor.

Dad turned and looked back at the person he'd passed coming in the front door. It was the lady of the house, vacuuming the carpet at nine in the morning in her nightgown. She stared at him for a few seconds and then said, "I bet you're looking for the radio station." My dad said, "Yes, ma'am. I sure am." She said, "Well, it moved. They got a new building uptown and my husband and I bought this one and it's now our home. We moved in last week."

My dad felt like a fool for bursting into this woman's house first thing in the morning. He had to say something, give her some kind of explanation, so on his way out the front door he introduced himself—as her United States senator, Alan Simpson.

Dad seemed to particularly enjoy telling this story whenever he was sharing stage with Senator Simpson, which happened quite often. They frequently appeared at the same events, and every two years, even though he wasn't up for re-election, Senator Simpson would campaign with my dad. He always said that it was to make sure that Dad didn't get any ideas about running for the Senate.

Senator Simpson didn't need to worry. Dad really enjoyed his time in the House of Representatives. He quickly moved into the Republican leadership, first as chairman of the Republican Policy Committee, then as chairman of the Republican Conference, and later as minority whip.

In 1988, he was asked to serve as chairman of the Rules Committee for the Republican National Convention in New Orleans. I was on summer break from college, and he asked me if I wanted to come with him and be a page at the convention. It sounded interesting, and the first few days were great, but when it was time to report to the Superdome for orientation, I quickly discovered that I was not cut out to be a page.

The first item on the agenda was clothing. The gentleman leading the session introduced two young people, a boy and a girl, who were modeling the convention-approved page uniform: for the boy, khaki pants, a white button-down shirt, and a red kerchief around the neck, and same for the girl, except that she was wearing a knee-length khaki skirt. The man described the uniform as comfortable, functional, and "youthfully professional," but I thought it looked disturbingly similar to the uniforms worn by the Young Pioneers, one of the Soviet Union's communist youth organizations.

After showing us what we would be wearing, the man told us about our duties. I had assumed that there would be a fair amount of scut work involved—making copies, painting signs, and handing out flyers—but I had also assumed that we would get to be on the floor of the convention, if only to take part in the demonstrations for the nominees. The man in charge informed us that while they would try to get us all on the floor at some point during the convention, they couldn't guarantee it.

That was enough for me. I left the orientation, resigned my position as a page, and scrounged up an extra set of floor credentials. Choosing between making copies in a windowless room in the basement of the Superdome while dressed like an aspiring communist and wearing what I wanted and being on the floor of the convention wasn't a real tough call. As an added bonus, not being a page freed up quite a bit of time in my schedule. I was nineteen, the drinking age in New Orleans was eighteen, and Bourbon Street was within easy walking distance of the hotel. It was a great convention.

In November 1988, Dad won a sixth term in the House. Trent Lott was moving over to the Senate, and my dad was elected to replace him as minority whip, the number-two position in the House. The Republicans hadn't been in control of the House for some forty years, but if and when they did take over, Dad was well positioned to become House Speaker. Things were about to turn pretty dramatically in another direction, however. The confirmation of John Tower, President George H. W. Bush's nominee to be secretary of defense, was in trouble. No one questioned whether the former four-term senator from Texas was qualified for the job, but there were allegations of drinking problems, womanizing, and improper ties to defense contractors. Rather than withdraw his name from nomination, Senator Tower stuck it out and was rejected by the Senate, 53–47. It was the first time that the Senate had ever rejected a new president's cabinet nominee.

On the day of the vote, when it became apparent that Senator Tower could not be confirmed, Dad was approached by two old friends, Jim Baker, the new secretary of state, and Brent Scowcroft, the national security advisor, about becoming secretary of defense. Given his service as a member of the House Select Committee on Intelligence and his focus on foreign policy and military affairs, he was more than qualified for the job, but Dad didn't immediately jump at the idea, though it certainly appealed to him. He wasn't in a big hurry to leave the House—he loved it there—but I think he felt he would always regret it if he didn't take on the challenge of the Defense Department. Besides, he'd always said that when the president asks you to take on an assignment, you're pretty much obligated to accept it, and that's what he did. The day after the Senate rejected John Tower, President George H. W. Bush nominated Dad to be his secretary of defense.

Dad's confirmation set all sorts of speed records. He was nominated on March 10, his confirmation hearing started on the fourteenth, and he was confirmed by a unanimous vote in the U.S. Senate and officially sworn in as secretary of defense on the seventeenth.

The official swearing in was a small ceremony held in my dad's congressional office, H104 in the Cannon House Office Building, and attended by my mom, Liz and me, and Dad's congressional staff—Dave Gribbin, Pete Williams, and Patty Howe, all from Wyoming, and Kathie Embody and Jim Steen, who had been working for my dad for years. The ceremony didn't take long, but our whole family could immediately see its impact.

As soon as the ceremony was over, Dad was surrounded by security personnel and military aides. My sister, Liz, says that's when she realized that everything had changed. He was no longer just one of 435 members of the House of Representatives. Now he was going to oversee all aspects of the U.S. military and be part of the chain of command. His congressional life, with its small, close-knit staff, had felt like part of our family life, but now we were going to have to share him with the whole country.

I remember watching through his office windows as security personnel ushered him into a waiting limousine and took him to his new office on the other side of the Potomac River. It was a remarkable change, and I was very proud of him.

I headed back to Colorado College, where I was a sophomore, thinking that however much my parents' lives had been upended, mine wouldn't really be any different, and if Saddam Hussein hadn't invaded Kuwait in August 1990, I might have actually been right. Colorado Springs, where Colorado College is located, is a conservative town, home to the Air Force Academy, Fort Carson, and lots of active duty and retired military personnel, but like most institutions of higher learning, Colorado College leans pretty hard to the left. The most outspoken faculty members were long-tenured professors who appeared to be still living quite happily in 1968. Through the build-up of Desert Shield and then with Desert Storm, there were a couple of antiwar protests at school, usually led by some of the more activist professors. I chose to express my opinion by having my mom send me a couple of sweatshirts that she found in Washington, D.C. They were black with big white letters that said "Free Kuwait." As I wore them around campus, I received many compliments from my fellow students, but I don't think they were all that popular with the more radical members of the faculty.

A small handful of students were rather vocal in their opposition to the Gulf War. One of the more enthusiastically antiwar members of my class wrote a column in the school paper suggesting that the best way to end the fighting would be to kidnap me and hold me hostage. I didn't take it all that seriously, but the police did. They provided me with a security detail and also made me temporarily move out of my off-campus apartment into the guest room of one of the detectives assigned to protect me. It wasn't how I planned on spending my last semester of college, but I understood that everyone wanted to err on the side of caution.

Once the war was over, the antiwar protesters moved their focus to graduation day. Dad had been invited to be the graduation speaker, and while most of the students and parents were looking forward to his speech, not everyone was. The school paper ran a political cartoon about two fictional Colorado College students, Love Child and Mountain Girl, who would be "transformed into blood thirsty demons of death" if Dad spoke at graduation. The cartoonist had obviously spent a great deal of time on the drawing, which made rather creative use of tie-dye and lightning bolts; subtle it wasn't.

When Dad was introduced as the graduation speaker, he got an enthusiastic response from the audience. The war was over, the United States had won, and the country was feeling good about itself and its leaders. But as my dad reached the podium, a majority of the faculty and a few students stood up and turned their backs to him, and they stayed that way throughout his speech. In case there was any confusion about their feelings, most of the protesters had scotch-taped paper peace signs or cutouts in the shape of doves onto their backs. As an added touch, a half dozen or so people stood around the perimeter of the ceremony wearing death masks and holding banners of protest—hard-to-read banners of protest, I might add. They'd crammed so much onto each one that none of them could be deciphered. The way I looked at it, if they were going to protest the graduation ceremony, the least they could do was use short, catchy, legible slogans.

I don't remember any protests about the Gulf War after graduation. Even on college campuses, they ran out of steam pretty quickly as people moved on to other issues, including the debate over the military's ban on gay and lesbian service members. It was a debate that would become very personal to me and to my family.

One of the military's primary arguments for banning gays was that they posed a security risk: Gay service members would be more susceptible to blackmail and coercion and therefore could not be trusted with matters of national security. By the early nineties this argument had been pretty well discredited, and it was widely accepted that gay soldiers didn't pose any greater security risk than straight ones. During a budget hearing in 1991, Congressman Barney Frank asked my dad about this argument. Dad described the policy as a "bit of an old chestnut," but while he didn't think gays and lesbians posed a security risk, he also wasn't pushing to change the Defense Department's policy. He was very clear in his belief that the job of the military is to defend the country, not to engage in social activism.

I understood and respected my father's position, but I disagreed with it. The ban hadn't prevented gays and lesbians from joining the armed forces. All it did was force gay and lesbian military personnel to hide their sexual orientation and force the military to spend time and money trying to root them out of the service. It was a bad policy. It was also a periodic topic of discussion at our family dinner table. I felt strongly about it, but I also felt strongly about what happened next.

It was the summer of 1991, and I was a recent college graduate and a lowly intern working for the U.S. Olympic Committee's National Sports Festival in Los Angeles. At the time, my biggest concern was whether the bus for the Tae Kwon Do competition was caught in rush hour traffic, but then my parents phoned to tell me that they'd both received calls at their offices from certain gay activists who were threatening to out me if the military didn't change its policy on gays. They also wanted me to know that there were reports that these same activists were shopping around a story about my being gay to several major media outlets. Since I wasn't a public figure, none of the outlets were picking the story up, but my parents wanted to give me a heads-up just in case.

It wasn't a secret that I was gay. I'd come out to my parents several years before during my junior year of high school on a day that is especially memorable because, in addition to being the day that I came out, it is also the day that I wrecked the family car when I was supposed to be in trigonometry. I had just broken up with my first girlfriend and was skipping class so I could run to the store and drown my sorrows in sugar. I was hurt, confused, and frustrated, and I didn't see the red light until it was too late. After I sorted out the insurance details from the car accident, I headed home. It was time to talk to my parents.

I have to admit that I'm not sure when I first knew that I was gay. There is no single moment in my life that I can point to and say, "That's when I knew." I think I always knew that there was something that made me different from most of my friends and classmates, and by the time I was in high school, I understood what it was. I was gay.

Unfortunately, it was the mid-1980s, and there weren't a lot of role models for gay teenagers. There were no gay student groups, and any teacher who happened to be gay had to stay in the closet or risk being fired. Mainstream news stories about gay men focused almost exclusively on the AIDS epidemic, and news stories about lesbians, when there were news stories about lesbians, were usually about Martina Navratilova and her complete dominance of the professional women's tennis circuit. There wasn't much that a sixteen-year-old girl with a lousy backhand could relate to.

When I got home, I told my mom that I'd had a car accident when I was supposed to be in school—and that I was gay. As soon as she figured out that I was being serious and not just offering the world's most creative excuse for a car accident, she hugged me and burst into tears. As I suppose most moms do, she had exalted notions of what I was capable of, of what I might accomplish with my life, and she worried about the limitations that a prejudiced society places on gay people. "Your life will be so hard," she said, but after I explained that my life would actually be much harder if I had to lie about who I was, she came to understand that society's reaction to my being gay was a secondary issue. I had to start with the fact that I'm gay and then deal with whatever the fallout was from people's prejudices after that.

When I told my dad, the first words out of his mouth were exactly the ones that I wanted to hear: "You're my daughter and I love you and I just want you to be happy." While we might not always agree on matters of policy, he has always been a loving and supportive father. Having heard stories about parents who have responded quite differently, I am very grateful to have the mother and father that I do.

Having loving and supportive parents, however, didn't make me feel any better about the possibility of seeing my personal life splashed across the newspapers and tabloids as part of the debate over gays in the military. And while I saw the activists' point that the military's policy needed to be changed, I strongly resented their using my sexual orientation in an attempt to blackmail my father. I also knew that it was just about the least effective strategy they could have chosen. My dad doesn't look kindly on threats, particularly if they are aimed at his family. Shortly after Dad left the Pentagon, a gay man whom he had known for several years came to see him at the American Enterprise Institute, where Dad had an office, and made some not-so-veiled threats about the publicity I would receive unless he spoke out about the military's policy on gays. Dad kicked him out of the office. The only thing threatening my dad ever accomplished was to make him angry.

These incidents were eye-openers for me. I had never imagined that there were people who would try to use me and my sexual orientation for their own political benefit. As far as I was concerned, they were lowlifes, pitiful lowlifes. But as I would discover in the 2004 campaign, they weren't alone. Some pretty high-profile people were willing to drag me into political debates simply because I'm my father's daughter and I happen to be gay.

When George H. W. Bush lost his bid for re-election in 1992, Dad left the Pentagon and gave serious consideration to running for president. He spent the 1994 election cycle traveling around the country giving speeches and doing over 160 fundraisers for Republican congressional candidates. That Christmas, we sat down as a family and discussed the possibility of his running for president in 1996, and, in the end, my dad decided that he really didn't want to do it. There's been speculation by Bob Woodward, among others, that one of the reasons he decided not to run was that he was worried about the attention that it would draw to me and to my private life. I've talked to my dad about it and he says it's simply not true. Ultimately, he decided not to run because he wasn't willing to do what you have to do if you want to be president. He didn't want to raise the money, travel endlessly, or worry whether every position he took was going to be popular in Iowa and New Hampshire.

We all assumed that this decision marked the end of his political career. None of us could have imagined that six years later he would be on the Republican ticket, running for vice president of the United States.

CHAPTER 3

The Personal Aide and Other Campaign Creatures

When I volunteered to help out on the 2000 campaign, I figured that I would be assigned to one of the advance teams that travel ahead of the candidate to set up rallies, speeches, and photo ops. Right out of college I'd spent a couple of years working for the Colorado Rockies baseball team and done everything from balloon launches and cannon salutes to opening days and parades, so I had a fair amount of experience putting on events, but advance work wasn't what my dad had in mind for me. Instead, he wanted me to be his personal aide.

Old school advance men refer to the personal aide as "the body guy." My dad described the job as being his "aide de camp." Whatever the job is called, it's a key position in any campaign. The personal aide is usually the first staff person to talk to the candidate in the morning and the last one to see him at night. He or she makes sure the candidate has his briefing papers, talking points, updated call list, and the names and bios of everyone who is greeting him when he lands at the next airport or arrives at the next rally.

When Dad asked me to be his personal aide, he explained that he needed not only someone who was smart, who had good judgment, and whom he could trust (all of which I took as a huge compliment), but also someone who knew him and understood how he worked. Unlike most national candidates, my dad was coming from the private sector, not the political world. That meant he didn't have a political staff to bring with him to the campaign. He was going to be surrounded by people who didn't know him and had never worked for him, so having a personal aide who did know him and understood how he worked would be a big help both for him and for the new staffers.

I was eager to take on the job. It would give me a front-row seat to the campaign, and it would allow me to travel with my parents. Best of all, it would continue our family's tradition of treating Dad's campaigns as family endeavors. And considering that one of my previous political jobs had been to stand on the corner outside Cheney for Congress headquarters wearing a sandwich board that said "Honk for Cheney," I figured personal aide had to be a promotion.

Dad suggested that I talk to Logan Walters, Governor Bush's personal aide. He'd been working for the governor for five years and had been his aide for the last three. If anyone knew the ins and outs of the job, it was Logan. Both Logan and his predecessor, Israel (Izzy) Hernandez, who now worked for Karl Rove, were kind enough to take the time to talk to me about what it takes to do the job well. As Logan and Izzy explained to me, there are basically five rules that all personal aides need to keep in mind.

1. No task is too big or too small. A personal aide has to be ready to do whatever the candidate needs so that the candidate can concentrate on campaigning. At the Republican National Convention in Philadelphia, the staff discovered that whenever we tried to cool down my parents' hotel room, the air-conditioning units would start dripping water down the walls and onto the floors, soaking the carpet and making the entire room reek of mildew. My parents were busy putting the finishing touches on Dad's convention speech. They didn't have time to deal with leaky air-conditioners, and the best efforts of the maintenance staff failed to fix the problem. Working with the hotel and the advance staff, I arranged for the staff to pull up the carpet every time my parents left their suite and bring in several large industrial fans to blow it dry. It was a bit noisy, but as long as we made sure there weren't any loose papers in the room before we turned the fans on, it worked.

2. Anticipate what the candidate will need. A good personal aide is always trying to figure out what's required for the next event, the next meeting, or the next plane ride. Anticipating the candidate's needs can be as simple as making sure he has his talking points for the next speech or as involved as trying to find a time and a place away from the cameras where he can practice throwing out the first pitch for a baseball game. Nobody, least of all the candidate, wants him to throw the ball in the dirt or over the backstop.

3. Carry a big bag. The candidate always needs to have his hands free so he can shake hands, wave at supporters, or pose for pictures. That means the personal aide has to carry everything. After the 2000 election, I emptied out the nylon bag I'd carried for three months on the campaign trail. It contained: two sets of briefing papers; the daily schedule for my dad; the daily schedule for Governor Bush; the monthly travel schedule; the daily news summary; the latest tracking polls; a cell phone; an extra cell phone battery; a cell phone battery charger; my dad's call list; phone directories for Bush campaign headquarters, the Republican National Committee, and Congress; personalized note cards; envelopes; stamps; a supply of Bush-Cheney campaign buttons and bumper stickers; two extra dress shirts (one white and one blue); two extra ties (one red and one blue); a comb; a bottle of hairspray; a bottle of sunscreen; and two tins of Altoids—cinnamon and mint.

At the very bottom of the bag were about a dozen Sharpies, felt-tip pins that make for fast and easy autographing, and several ballpoint pens for autographing objects that Sharpies don't work well on—like baseballs. The other item I had in abundance was hand sanitizer, a half dozen small bottles of it. A good personal aide has one at the ready as soon as the candidate finishes a photo op or a ropeline. A reporter who once saw Dad use hand sanitizer after he'd been shaking hands made a thing of it, as though it somehow indicated an aversion to retail politics. The truth is, all candidates use it—or suffer the consequences. When Wesley Clark entered the 2004 presidential race, he caught a cold, lost his voice, and was unable to campaign for several days. Some people speculated that the pace of a national campaign had knocked the former NATO commander off the campaign trail. I knew it was because he hadn't learned about hand sanitizer. National candidates shake hundreds, if not thousands, of hands every day. They will get sick unless they wash their hands early and often.

4. Be anonymous. Logan Walters put it best: "Always be within earshot, but out of the photo shot." The personal aide has to be nearby in case the candidate needs something, but good personal aides find ways to stick close without drawing attention to themselves. The focus of the press and everyone else should be on the candidate, not the staff. It sounded simple enough, and I thought it would be relatively easy to operate under the radar of the media. I soon discovered how wrong I was. One morning at the convention in Philadelphia I woke up to the sound of someone banging on the door of my hotel room. Bleary-eyed and in my pajamas, I opened the door to find a member of the advance staff holding up a copy of *USA Today*. There was my picture on the front page over the caption "Cheney in the spotlight." The story was about me, my sexual orientation, and whether it would be an issue for the campaign. At that point, I realized that remaining anonymous might not be quite as easy as I had thought.

5. Stay on schedule. I've read about how it never seemed to bother Bill Clinton to keep people waiting, but Governor Bush and my dad thought it was rude. It ties up traffic because the police have to shut down streets for longer periods of time, and it also tends to annoy the traveling media, since one of the easiest ways to make up time in the schedule is to cut the time the press gets for filing their stories. Staying on schedule was mandatory, not just for the personal aides, but for everyone working on the Bush-Cheney campaign.

The personal aide is the staffer who is responsible for trying to keep the candidate on time, which in my dad's case wasn't usually that difficult. But every once in a while, like all politicians, he'd get caught up in an event and it would run overtime, but then I'd put my hand in the air, he'd get the idea, take one more question from the audience, and wrap things up.

Every now and then, though, he would present me with a challenge. The speech would be going just right, the audience would be cheering in all the right spots, whooping and hollering and shouting encouragement to him, and he wouldn't want to stop. He conveniently wouldn't see me when I was signaling him from the buffer zone—the area down on the floor in front of the stage that was reserved for Secret Service agents and photographers—so I'd move a little closer to the podium and try again. If he continued to ignore me, I'd climb up on the press platform, stand behind the cameras, and jump up and down. I could see my mom up on the stage smiling at my many methods, but sooner or later one of them would work.

I was always on the lookout for a surefire way to get his attention, and on the last weekend of the 2000 campaign I found one. We were barnstorming through Wisconsin on a beautiful, crisp fall day, doing a series of airport rallies with Bart Starr, the legendary Green Bay Packers quarterback. The crowds were big. People were cheering, waving signs, and laughing at my dad's jokes. He was having a blast, which meant he was also totally ignoring my signals. We were running pretty late, so when we got to La Crosse, I decided it was time for drastic measures.

I found the barbershop quartet that had been entertaining the crowd before our arrival. This being football season in Wisconsin, they were all wearing foam rubber cheesehead hats. After several minutes of negotiating, I talked them into selling me one. I put it on, walked back into the buffer zone, and stood directly in my dad's line of sight.

He was well into his stump speech and on a roll. He was letting the audience have it with both barrels, and they loved it. Then, in midsentence, Dad looked down, saw me standing there with a piece of yellow foam rubber cheese on my head, and he broke up. By the time he quit laughing, he'd lost track of where he was in his speech. He turned to my mom, who fortunately had been paying attention. She gave him the next line, and he took it from there, wrapped up the speech, worked the ropeline, and we headed for the next stop, nearly back on schedule. It would have made life a whole lot easier if I'd come up with the cheesehead solution earlier in the campaign.

One of the best parts of being a personal aide is that you get to interact with all the different types of people who work on a campaign. The policy types tend to be introverted and on the quiet side, but they are really, really smart, and, in the case of our policy guys, smart enough not to be arrogant about it. They know everything there is to know about the economy or energy or national defense—though they can be a little weak on history and abysmal when it comes to popular culture, as I discovered during a couple of games of Trivial Pursuit. They could explain down to the penny the impact Governor Bush's tax plan would have on any given American family, but none of them knew who Chachi was.

The communications people are outgoing, clever, and even-tempered enough to deal with the media. Karen Hughes, the communications director in 2000 and a senior advisor in 2004, was truly amazing in the intelligent and forceful way she presented policy positions and deftly handled questions. She had the respect of the reporters covering the campaign, and she never, ever confused her job with being their friend.

The political staff are responsible for building coalitions, recruiting volunteers, and driving the get-out-the-vote effort on Election Day. They tend to be organized, high-energy, and willing and able to talk about precinct voter goals for hours on end. Ken Mehlman, the national field director in 2000 and the Bush-Cheney '04 campaign manager, is the most evolved form of the political type I've ever worked with. He is tireless, able to recite the most obscure political facts about county voting trends and population growth, and he can tell you the number of registered Republican voters in any given precinct in the state of Ohio. Ken can perpetually juggle at least a dozen different projects; everything from overseeing ballot access in key battleground states, to building coalitions of Hispanic voters in the Southwest, to energizing and motivating young campaign staffers and volunteers. Just watching him work is exhausting.

But while every department in a campaign has a different feel and seems to attract a different personality type, the real dividing line on a campaign isn't between the different departments like communications and policy. It's between those staffers who are members of the cult and those who aren't.

The cult is the cult of advance men and women, the staff who go into a city three to five days ahead of the candidate and set up an event, doing everything from building the staging and installing the sound system to working with the Secret Service and White House Communications. I don't know who first called advance people "the cult," but it's a term I heard in both 2000 and 2004, and I have to admit, it fits. Advance staffers have their own culture and even their own lore—legendary tales of advance work that have been passed down over the years.

I suppose I know these stories as well as any nonmember of the cult because I grew up hearing them. One of my dad's oldest and dearest friends is Ron Walker, who, as director of advance for President Nixon, wrote the first manual outlining all the rules of effective advance work. This wasn't some bureaucratic, dry-as-dust handbook. While it laid out procedures and rules for advancing presidential events, including step-by-step directions for how to create the most photogenic balloon release (use a parachute instead of a net to hold the balloons), it also included an entire page on hats emphasizing that under no circumstances should President Nixon ever be presented with a hat to wear. This was such an important rule that the last line of the manual was "HATS ARE TOXIC AND CAN KILL YOU." A "no hats" rule may sound like an odd one, but it's actually pretty important. Very few candidates look good, much less presidential, wearing any type of hat. All you have to do is look at a picture of Michael Dukakis in the army helmet or John Kerry in the biosuit to understand why most campaigns stay as far away from hats as they can.

During the 1976 presidential campaign, someone was always presenting President Ford with some odd piece of headgear. He never wanted to offend anyone, so he'd put the hat on and, invariably, a bad photo would appear in the next day's newspapers. As chief of staff, my dad told the advance staff to do whatever they needed to do to pre-empt further hat incidents. One creative advance team saved the day by seizing a raccoon skin hat that someone was about to give to President Ford and nailed it to an old bread board so that there was no possible way that the president could put it on.

Mike Duval, another friend of my father's who did advance for Nixon and Ford, had a great story about how good advance saved a national secret—after nearly exposing it. Mike was sent to California with instructions to set up a ceremony for a maritime-bill signing in a shipyard. He headed for San Diego, but when he got there, he discovered it was a slow time for building ships. He could find only one ship under construction. He noticed that it looked kind of odd, but figured that it would do for the event. He brought in a press platform, lighting, and power. He arranged everything down to the smallest detail, but the night before the event, he got a call from the National Security Council telling him that under no circumstances could the ship be shown in any photograph. They didn't tell him why, just told him to make sure it didn't happen.

It was too late to move the event, so Mike did the next best thing: He moved the press platform. Using one of the cranes in the shipyard he had the press platform brought so close to the ship that all any photo would show was a solid steel wall. To further obscure the ship, he placed part of the crane in the shot and had several shipyard employees in hard hats sit on it. The ship was completely unrecognizable, and the event went off without a hitch.

It wasn't until several years later that Mike understood why he had been told not to show the ship. He saw a front-page news story about a top secret CIA operation to raise a damaged Soviet sub off the floor of the Pacific Ocean. The CIA had quietly contracted to build a special ship for the mission, the *Glomar Explorer*. Mike looked at the photo and realized that it was the same odd-looking ship he'd spotted in the San Diego shipyard.

Advance work has changed a lot over the years. In the early days, advance teams were fairly autonomous, self-contained units. They had to be. Without email, cell phones, fax machines, or FedEx, it was impossible for staff at campaign headquarters to oversee an event taking place clear across the country. The only way to make an event work was to dispatch an advance team that would be responsible for everything: choosing the venue; setting up the staging, lighting, and sound; and contacting local supporters and media to help build the crowds.

The introduction of cell phones, the internet, and digital photography has allowed a lot of the initial decision-making regarding events to shift back to campaign headquarters. Now, the site is picked; local political leaders contacted; and banners, posters, and brochures selected and approved before an advance person ever reaches town. Campaign finance laws have also changed advance work a great deal. I've heard stories about the days before campaign finance regulations, when advance men were sent out on the road with a suitcase full of cash and one instruction, "Get it done." It's not quite that simple anymore. In today's general elections, each campaign has a fixed amount of money to spend and strict rules regarding how it can spend it. This means that the staff at head-quarters is watching every dollar to ensure that the campaign is making the most effective use of its resources and staying well within the law.

This doesn't always sit well with the advance types, who have "get it done" engraved on their frontal lobes—or else they wouldn't be in advance work. They've been known to regard the people at headquarters as a bunch of obstructionists who can easily be ig-nored, so they might triple an event budget without checking with anyone at campaign headquarters, or decide that what the rally really needs is an eighty-thousand-dollar closed-circuit TV system so that the supporters waiting in the gym can watch the candidate's car pull into the dark alley behind the school. The advance staff spends the money without permission, the person in charge back at headquarters goes crazy, angry phone calls and emails are exchanged, and the idea that there are really only two basic political types in any campaign—those who are in the cult and those who aren't—takes firmer hold.

Maddening as advance people can be, they are essential to a successful operation. People have gotten used to well-put-together events where the flags are flying, the music is playing, and the crowds are pumped. These things have to happen for a campaign to look successful, and they don't happen by accident. Good advance work gets the credit—a point that becomes particularly clear when, as happens every once in a while, the advance work isn't quite so good.

It was September 2000, and we had just touched down in Fresno, California. The campaign had arranged to hold a welcome rally at the airport. It was supposed to be a small event, just a few brief remarks to the crowd so we could get some footage of Dad delivering the message of the day on the local news.

The advance team came on board the plane to brief my parents about the program. A local VIP was going to introduce my mom, who would then introduce my dad, they explained. Dad, meanwhile, was looking out the plane window trying to see where he was supposed to stand to deliver his remarks. "Where's the microphone?" he asked. And that's when we learned that we didn't have one.

The advance team had worked with the local political staff to ensure we had a good crowd and arranged to use the "Bush-Cheney" plane as the backdrop for the photo shot, but they forgot about a sound system. Given that we discovered this fact a mere thirty seconds before my parents were to walk off the plane, there was no way to fix the problem. Mom and Dad got off the plane, shook some hands, and waved good-bye as though that's what had been planned all along. They drove off, leaving an only slightly puzzled crowd standing on the tarmac.

The men and women who do political advance work come from a wide variety of backgrounds. When they're not being advance people, they teach school, trade bonds, work for insurance companies, do public speaking, and run event-planning companies. And the very best of them share a common conviction: They know they can get the job done, no matter how impossible it may seem.

In late 2003, Dad was scheduled to speak at a luncheon fundraiser in New York City. Because most of the attendees would be Jewish, the campaign arranged to have a rabbi offer a prayer before the event. As *Air Force Two* was en route to New York, I called the lead advance person to make sure that everything was set. It was, she said—except there was a small problem with the rabbi. She'd just called him to confirm time and location only to have him tell her that he was on his way to the hospital for emergency surgery. It was nothing serious, she said, but we definitely needed a new rabbi, and she assured me that she would have one there in plenty of time. Given that there wasn't much I could do about the situation at thirty-five thousand feet, I just had to hope that she was right. She was. By the time we arrived at the luncheon, she'd located a new rabbi and got him to the event and cleared through the Secret Service and the White House with plenty of time to spare.

Advance people have a lot of self-confidence. Some of them may even have a bit too much, but that also is part of their lore. Consider the story of the advance men who were preparing for a presidential trip to the Soviet Union during the Cold War. After a long day spent arguing with their Soviet hosts about meeting sites, seating arrangements, and other protocol issues, they retired to their room taking at least one, but more likely several, bottles of vodka with them. The team knew their room was bugged, and after a few drinks, they decided that they were going to find the listening devices.

They started small, looking behind all the paintings and mirrors, but nothing was there. Next, they took apart the lamps and light fixtures, and even dismantled the toilet, but they still couldn't find anything. Finally, they moved all the furniture and rolled back the rug. That's when they found it—a metal plate held down by four screws. They knew they were close. It took a while to undo the screws, but they stuck with it and finally removed the plate. Underneath it, they saw a bunch of wires and a single bolt, which was firmly in place, but little by little they managed to twist it off—and that's when they, and everyone else in the hotel, heard a terrible crash. They had unscrewed the chandelier in the banquet room below.

CHAPTER 4

The Bubble

July 25, 2000, was the last day my dad got to drive his car. In his seven-year-old STS, he drove himself and my mom to Love Field in Dallas, Texas, where they got on a plane for Austin—and a whole new way of life. Once Governor Bush formally announced my dad as his running mate, my parents would become protectees of the Secret Service, which meant they would never drive or go anywhere by themselves and they would never ever leave "the bubble."

Technically, "the bubble" refers to the perimeter of security that the Secret Service sets up around protectees, particularly around the president, the vice president, and the national parties' nominees for those offices, but over the years, "being inside the bubble" has also come to refer to the peculiar way of life adopted by the people living within it.

The protectee, or principal, is at the center of the bubble, but he or she isn't the only resident. Others include: family members and staff that accompany the principal, Secret Service agents, the traveling press corps, and important guests who might come along on the road for a few days; basically, anyone who is part of the principal's traveling party. In the case of a president or a presidential nominee hundreds of individuals may be "inside the bubble," all of whom have special identification and follow a specific set of security procedures.

The Secret Service agents assigned to my parents in 2000 were professional, courteous, respectful, and as accommodating as they could possibly be. The leader of my dad's detail, Chuck Wofford, took time to explain how the Secret Service operates and the steps that the agents would take to ensure my parents' safety. He also warned us that it would probably take some time to adjust to the new arrangements. He was right. Even though Dad had had a security detail assigned to him when he was secretary of defense, it wasn't nearly as thorough or as elaborate as what the Secret Service provides to a nominee for vice president.

A few days after the announcement, we were in Washington, D.C., getting ready to fly up to the Republican National Convention in Philadelphia. While my parents were getting ready for the convention—packing, working on my dad's acceptance speech, and making lists of the friends and family they wanted to invite to Philadelphia—the Secret Service set up a temporary headquarters in the garage of their townhouse.

A protectee's schedule is of vital importance to the Secret Service, who plan motorcade routes, shift changes, and travel arrangements around it. That's why one of the first things the Secret Service asks for is a schedule of upcoming events and travel. But when my dad was first announced as the nominee, he didn't have a campaign staff, and there wasn't anyone who was responsible for providing a schedule to the Secret Service. That left the agents scrambling to get the information any way that they could, which meant a barrage of scheduling questions for any nonagent who happened to walk through the garage—which usually meant Liz and me.

Every time either one of us walked through the garage, all the agents would start asking questions. "Is he going to the grocery store?" "Do you have a departure time yet for Philadelphia?" "Are they going out to dinner tonight?" "Is she going to the dry cleaners?" Usually, our answer was, "I don't know." We weren't trying to be difficult or to withhold information. We understood and appreciated that the agents were just trying to do their jobs, but we honestly didn't know the answers.

Unfortunately, saying we didn't know the answer only led to more questions: "What are their plans for tonight?" "Is he going to the dry cleaners?" "Do you think they'll want to leave for Philadelphia in the morning or the afternoon?" "Are they going to be OK with a 6:30 A.M. baggage call?" I wasn't even sure what a baggage call was, much less what time it should be. (For the record, it's the time when all luggage is given to the agents so that it can be secured and transferred to the plane.) It was like going through a mini-interrogation every time we tried to enter or leave the house. Liz and I started referring to the experience as running "The Gauntlet of Curiosity."

Scheduling issues aside, adjusting to life inside the bubble presented a whole series of challenges. The more obvious changes, such as my parents' no longer driving themselves, were relatively easy to get used to. The tough ones were the changes that no one warned us about. At the Philadelphia convention, one of the most unexpected challenges we faced was getting food. Liz was the first to notice the problem. She and her husband, Phil, had brought their three daughters to the convention: Kate, age six; Elizabeth, age three; and Grace, age four months. On the first morning Liz called room service and ordered pancakes for the two older girls. She got the kids dressed, then walked down to Mom and Dad's room to find out what the plans were for the day. I was already there and the four of us talked for a while, then Liz went to check on the kids. Instead of eating breakfast, they were rolling around on the floor at the far end of the hallway, wailing in a rather pitiful way, "We're hungry! Where are our pancakes?" Room service had told Liz it would take only fifteen to twenty minutes. It was now an hour later, so Liz called down to the kitchen and was told that the server had left with her order quite a while ago. Thinking that it might have been delivered to one of the other rooms on the floor, she asked the agents posted outside our parents' room if they'd seen a room service cart. They hadn't, but one of them told her that the elevators were turned off so that no one could get to our floor without a Secret Service escort. Room service couldn't reach us. Liz went down the elevator with one of the agents and found the pancakes. They were a little cold, but at least the girls got their breakfast, and our family learned an important lesson about life inside the bubble: If we wanted to order food, calling room service wasn't enough. We had to tell the agents as well.

Learning that lesson, however, didn't solve all of our food problems. My parents were incredibly busy at the convention. When they weren't attending an event, they were rehearsing my dad's acceptance speech on the teleprompter the campaign had set up in the hotel. They didn't have much down time, so I tried to preorder all of their meals. I even made sure to notify the Secret Service so there wouldn't be any repeats of the pancake incident. The problem was that no matter what I did, no matter how many people I told, about half the time, the food just wouldn't show up. It was bizarre.

I'd call the kitchen and they'd tell me that the food had been sent up. They'd even tell me the exact time that it was delivered. I'd explain that while I appreciated their attention to detail, I still didn't have the food. Eventually, I'd give up and place another order. Without fail, the second order would always arrive right on time. I couldn't figure out what the problem was.

The mystery was finally solved on the last day of the convention. As usual, I'd preordered lunch for my parents, but when we arrived back at the hotel after Dad's morning events it wasn't in their room. Frustrated, I called down to the kitchen. The woman who answered the phone explained that the lunch had been delivered over a half hour ago. I explained that that was impossible, that there were agents posted outside the hotel room and that I was sure they would have noticed if someone had dropped off a room service cart. After several minutes, we both realized that the meal had been delivered not to my parents' room, but to Governor Bush's.

It turned out that all of the missing food had been delivered to Governor Bush's suite. Whenever we ordered for my parents, if it was close to the governor's mealtime, our food would somehow be intercepted and sent to him. This would happen even if my parents' order was completely different from what the governor had asked for.

I never did figure out who diverted the food, but the experience reinforced an important fact about life inside the bubble: While the vice presidential nominee is important, he is the number-two person on the ticket, a key consideration to keep in mind, particularly around mealtime.

There are lots of people, both politicians, and nonpoliticians, who are obsessed with whether they have the best hotel suite, the largest entourage, or the best table for lunch. They would have been absolutely furious to discover that their food had been rerouted, even if it had gone to the presidential nominee. Fortunately, Dad isn't one of these people. He is one of the least ego-driven people I have ever met, and when he found out what had been happening to the food, instead of getting angry, he joked that it was probably part of an elaborate plot to make sure he was watching his diet.

When Dad wasn't scavenging for food or preparing for his acceptance speech, he was interviewing people for some of his key positions on the campaign. The first order of business was to find a chief of staff, someone who could oversee the VP side of the campaign operation. At the top of everyone's lists was a woman named Kathleen Shanahan. She had worked in the Reagan and Bush White Houses, was close to the Bush family, and had a reputation for being smart, tough, and totally competent. Dad asked her to come by the hotel to discuss the job, and as his personal aide, I was supposed to meet her downstairs and bring her up to the suite. Not having the slightest idea what she looked like, I stood in the hallway outside the staff office and scanned faces, trying to figure out who might be named Kathleen. She was impossible to miss: bright red hair, wearing a lime green suit, and radiating a force field of energy. I liked her immediately, as did the rest of the family. She became Dad's campaign chief of staff, as well as a good family friend.

Dad filled a few other key positions during the convention. Jay Parmer agreed to serve as the tour director. A former director of advance for Vice President George H. W. Bush, Jay would oversee all of Dad's travel and event arrangements. Marguerite Sullivan, a longtime friend of my mom's from her days at the National Endowment for the Humanities, came on board as her chief of staff, and Stephanie Lundberg, who had worked for her at the American Enterprise Institute, became her personal aide. Lea Berman and Laura Chadwick, who had been indispensable at the convention, continued as invaluable volunteers, willing to do anything from advancing an event to finding babysitters. We still didn't have a permanent press secretary to travel with us, but at least Liz and I were no longer the only non–Secret Service agents traveling with our parents. We now had some company inside the bubble, and Dad no longer had to worry about things like when the plane would take off or whether he had the right talking points for the next reception. He could focus on campaigning. It was a marked improvement. But having staff also meant adjusting to being surrounded by people who would jump into action at the slightest hint from my parents. That took some getting used to. It meant that my parents, and to a lesser extent Liz and I, had to be careful about the messages that we sent to the staff, particularly unintended ones.

When they lived in Dallas, my parents had a regular morning routine. Every morning, Dad would drive down to the local coffee shop to pick up lattes and newspapers. But now that he and Mom were protectees of the Secret Service, Dad couldn't just run out for coffee. Agents, advance men, local police, and a phalanx of cameras would all be involved.

To help my parents out at the convention, a young volunteer named Brian McCormack offered to run out for lattes first thing every morning. It seemed like the best solution and worked really well for the first couple of days, but one day there was a morning rush at Starbucks, and Brian got stuck in line.

Dad popped his head into the staff office at about 6:30 A.M. and asked if anyone knew where the coffee was. He wasn't upset. He just wanted to make sure that it was on its way. He was assured that it was. Someone in the staff office then called Brian on his cell phone to tell him to hurry up. Brian explained that he was doing the best that he could, but that there was a long line and that it was probably going to be a while before he got back to the hotel. This spurred the rest of the staff into action.

When Brian finally got back to the hotel, he went straight to Mom and Dad's suite. He figured my parents would be glad to see him, even if he was a little late, but when he walked in, Dad looked up from his newspaper, fixed Brian with an over-the-glasses stare, and said in an unmistakably irritated voice, "No more lattes!"

Confused, Brian said, "Yes, sir," and turned to leave, but before he could get out the door, he heard my mom's voice coming from another room. "If those are lattes, just put them on the table with the others. We'll drink them eventually." That was when Brian noticed at least a dozen "to-go" cups sitting on the table by the door.

Rather than wait for Brian to return, the rest of the staff had taken matters into their own hands and judging by the variety of cups on the table, it looked like they had gone to every coffee outlet within a ten-block radius of the hotel. There were enough lattes in my parents' suite to caffeinate an office full of people.

While my parents, particularly my mom, didn't mind a few extra lattes, this episode was a reminder of how tuned in the staff was to everything they said. Dad hadn't meant for anyone else to go out and get coffee, and he certainly hadn't intended for everyone to go out and get it, but that's what happened—all because he'd asked where the coffee was.

In retrospect, it shouldn't have been all that surprising. When you are the principal living inside the bubble, surrounded by agents and staff, people have a tendency to want to stay on your good side. It's a potential pitfall that anyone who lives inside the bubble has to deal with, particularly since it means that people will often tell the principal what they think he wants to hear rather than what he needs to hear.

Dad, who has been a staffer himself, has talked about how this phenomenon can appear from the staff side. When he was Gerald Ford's chief of staff, people would call him up and say they had an urgent matter that they had to see the president about. Maybe it was something they thought the president was doing wrong on the economy or perhaps they wanted to tell him about growing discontent among some group of Republican voters. Whatever it was, they thought it was of great importance, and so my dad would set up an appointment for them, but when they walked into the Oval Office, they'd ask President Ford how Betty and the kids were and how his golf game was going. They'd bring up everything except the urgent issue, which they just couldn't bring themselves to address while sitting in the Oval Office talking to the president of the United States. No one wanted to be the bearer of bad news. After the meeting, they would come down to my dad's office and lay the matter on him. "You've just got to get the president to do something," they'd say. So now Dad made it very clear to his staff that he appreciated people who gave him frank, unvarnished information. And, of course, he also had my mother, my sister, and me, three people who never hesitate to tell him exactly what we think.

Not long after Dad was sworn in for his first term as vice president, Mom joked about how hard it is to get a frank opinion once you've achieved an elevated political status. She was at a prayer breakfast in Washington, D.C., when the person sitting next to her asked how her life had changed. "It's hard to get a good disagreement going anymore," she laughed. After the breakfast, a woman who had been sitting several seats away introduced herself to my mom, and said, "I live in your neighborhood, and if you ever need anybody to disagree with you, I'd be glad to come over." It was Elizabeth Edwards, wife of Senator John Edwards from North Carolina. My mom was a little taken aback, but she smiled politely, observing later that in Washington nothing brings politics to a halt—not even a breakfast dedicated to prayer.

One other aspect of life inside the bubble that caught all of us a bit by surprise was the complete loss of privacy. While we all expected that Dad's nomination would result in some loss, I don't think any of us understood just how total it would be. By the end of the convention, I realized that most of the staff and all of the agents had seen me wearing the pajama bottoms and the University of Colorado T-shirt that I slept in. I was getting only four to five hours of sleep a night, but when you are surrounded by staff and agents twenty-four hours a day, people knock on your door at odd hours to give you the latest briefing papers or to ask questions about a breaking news story. At first, it seemed a little odd to have a conversation in my pajamas about an upcoming speech or event, but it quickly got to the point where it just stopped registering. Maybe it was because I was so busy and so tired, but I just resigned myself to the fact that with all of these people constantly around, they were bound to see me looking much less than my very best.

Even with all the lessons we had to learn and the adjustments we had to make, the convention in Philadelphia was an amazing experience. We were surrounded by friends like Ann and Al Simpson, Dave and Karen Nicholas, and Don and Joyce Rumsfeld. They were all there to support us the night of Dad's acceptance speech, and the crowd could not have been more positive or enthusiastic.

Mom went onstage first to introduce Dad. She'd written her speech herself and decided that instead of focusing on my dad's impressive résumé, she wanted to introduce him by telling stories about him that most people didn't know, stories about how as a young boy he used to love visiting his grandfather, a cook on the Union Pacific Railroad; about how when we were little, he used to take me and Liz to tour Civil War battlefields, sharing with us his lifelong love of history. Finally, she explained that one of the keys to understanding Dick Cheney is understanding the sport of fly-fishing. She said, "It's not a sport for the impatient. And, most of all, it's not a sport for chatterboxes." Nobody knows my dad better than she does, and she gave him a terrific introduction.

Then it was Dad's turn. My parents had spent long hours working with John McConnell and Matt Scully, two of the Bush campaign's very talented speechwriters. Mom remembered that during his 1992 convention speech, Al Gore had said of President George H. W. Bush and Vice President Quayle, "It's time for them to go." She remembered how powerful the line had been—and how irritating. She thought it would be perfect to have Dad turn the line on Al Gore and Bill Clinton in 2000.

Initially, there was some resistance from a few members of the senior staff back in Austin. They pointed out that all of the other convention speakers were going to be very positive. They were going to talk about all of the good things that George W. Bush had done as governor and all that he would accomplish as president. They weren't eager to have anyone aggressively criticize Bill Clinton or Al Gore. Ultimately, my dad did what he always does: He listened to everyone's advice and then decided to give the speech that he wanted to give. He talked about the characteristics and qualities that make a great president, about seeing those qualities in presidents like Ronald Reagan, Gerald Ford, and George H. W. Bush, and about seeing those qualities in Governor Bush. He criticized the squandered opportunities of the Clinton-Gore administration and laid out the case against giving Al Gore four more years in Washington, D.C. The delegates loved it.

Dad's speech was the first real red meat of the convention, and the audience couldn't get enough. They cheered every sentence. They started chanting lines from the speech like "It's time for them to go" and "Help is on the way." They stamped their feet, clapped their hands, and yelled and cheered all the way through. It was so loud inside the arena that you could actually feel the noise.

Dad had to stop several times to let the crowd settle down so he could be heard. He told us later that at one point he looked down at the California delegation and saw former secretary of state George Shultz, a man not known for getting overly excited, chanting and cheering right along with the rest of the crowd. It was a great speech.

The last event of the night was the closing prayer. Earlier in the day, Mom, being a mom, had warned me and Liz that there would probably be cameras on us during the prayer and that, no matter what, we were supposed to keep our eyes closed and our heads down. In the manner of daughters everywhere, we both rolled our eyes and said, "We know. We know."

Liz had brought her two oldest daughters, Kate and Elizabeth, to watch Dad's speech, and the girls were great all the way through the evening. They loved the confetti and balloons released at the end of the speech. All we had to do was make it through the closing prayer and we could go congratulate Mom and Dad on the great job that they'd done.

A few seconds into the prayer, I heard what sounded like a dog barking. I kept my head down, but peeked over and saw Elizabeth, the three-year-old, leaning over the railing of the box, barking at the reporters and photographers gathered below. I knew this was not a good thing for her to be doing, but wasn't sure how to stop her without making it worse. Head still bent, I whispered to Liz, "What should we do?" She said, "I don't know. I don't want to grab her. That will just draw more attention." Liz and I tried whispering at Elizabeth to get her to stop barking, which only seemed to encourage her. She barked some more, and every time she did, more photographers showed up. Liz and I couldn't help ourselves. We started laughing.

Backstage all Mom could see on the television feed was Liz and me talking and laughing when we were supposed to be listening to the closing prayer. Appalled, she asked herself that most elemental question of mothers everywhere: What kind of children have I raised? Later we got Elizabeth to demonstrate her bark for my mom so that she would understand that Liz and I were innocent victims of circumstance.

One other occasion from the convention that really stands out for me wasn't a public event, it was a private meeting that my dad had with former president Ford. As Dad's personal aide, I went with him to the former president's hotel.

As always, President Ford was incredibly gracious. He put his arm around my shoulder and asked me if I was proud of my father. I said, "Yes, sir, Mr. President. I am." He said, "Good, I am, too." Dad was standing across the room, but I could see him smile and knew how much it meant to have President Ford say that.

My dad has always admired and respected President Ford as a decent and honorable man and a good president. His pardon of Richard Nixon was one of the most politically unpopular decisions in our country's history. It probably cost him the election in 1976, but it was the right thing to do. In a time of national crisis, Gerald Ford put the country's interests ahead of his own.

After the meeting, on the ride back to our hotel, Dad talked to me about President Ford and the chance that he had taken by naming my dad to be his chief of staff. Dad was only thirty-four years old at the time, wasn't well known in Washington, and had never held a major political post, but President Ford gave him the opportunity to show what he could do. Dad also talked about all of the other people who had given him opportunities during his career. People like Don Rumsfeld, who had hired him in 1969 to run legislative affairs at the Office of Economic Opportunity and Bill Steiger, a congressman from Wisconsin who gave him his very first job in Washington, D.C. I thought how characteristic it was for him to be thinking not about himself but about people who'd helped him along the way. Here he was at the Republican National Convention, surrounded by Secret Service agents and staff, getting ready to run a national campaign as the vice presidential nominee. Everything in his life might be changing, but nothing was going to change him.

CHAPTER 5

Nine Days of Hell

When we left the Philadelphia convention on August 4, most polls showed Governor Bush holding a double-digit lead over Vice President Gore. Four weeks later, after the Democratic convention and going into the Labor Day weekend, the polls showed either a tie or a slim lead for Vice President Gore. We knew we had to get on offense and turn the race around. What we didn't know was that our troubles would multiply before our campaign regained momentum, and that in the week or so after Labor Day, we would hit an especially bad stretch, a time I'd forever after refer to as the "nine days of hell."

During the convention, Karl Rove had come up to my parents' suite and given our family and some of the staff a PowerPoint presentation on where things stood and what the plans were for the fall campaign. He pointed to all the states where we were leading and told us that if the election were held right then, we'd "roll up well over three hundred electoral votes." Karl explained that the strategy for the general election was to compete not only in traditional battleground states such as Missouri and Ohio, but also in established Democratic strongholds like California.

Traditionally, vice presidential candidates are dispatched to safe states where their job is to fire up the base and hammer away at the opposition, but Karl made it clear that this campaign would be different. Rather than campaigning in safe Republican states like Alabama and Oklahoma, Dad would mostly travel to the battleground states. That way the campaign could cover more of the territory that really mattered and get on the air in more key media markets. Travel schedules for Dad and Governor Bush would be based on a combination of overnight tracking polls, county-specific voter goals, and requests from local party leaders. But it took us a long time to get started on this plan. With the exception of a few fundraisers and some joint appearances with Governor Bush, my dad's travel schedule didn't really kick in until the end of August. There were a couple of reasons for this. First and foremost was that we didn't have a plane.

For the last few months, Governor Bush had been traveling on a chartered 727. After the convention, the plan was for him to fly on a bigger plane that could accommodate more traveling press and for Dad to take over the 727. Unfortunately, the new plane wasn't ready yet, and until it was, the governor would have the 727, and my dad would use a much smaller Gulfstream. There was no room for traveling press, and we quickly understood that one sure way to make reporters even grumpier than they normally are was to not take them along on a campaign swing. If we wanted to keep press hostility down, we reasoned, better not to go to too many places.

Another factor was that the Democratic National Convention was scheduled for the middle of August. Traditionally, presidential and vice presidential candidates refrain from campaigning during the other party's convention, so Dad planned to spend that week at home in Jackson, Wyoming, reading policy papers and getting up to speed on issues before going out to campaign full-time.

While we were waiting to hit the campaign trail, the Gore campaign had a great month. Vice President Gore got a sizeable boost in the polls coming out of his convention and the media couldn't get enough of his running mate, Senator Joe Lieberman of Connecticut. Senator Lieberman's press coverage was incredibly positive. Stories described him as the first Jewish vice presidential candidate, a man of honor and integrity, and they always mentioned his humble beginnings as the son of a bakery truck driver. When Governor Bush announced my dad as his running mate at the end of July, there were a few nice comments in the press about what a steady, responsible leader he was. I remember that Colin Powell said something thoughtful and positive. But the general contrast to the press commentary about Joe Lieberman could not have been greater. As *USA Today* saw it, Vice President Gore's pick signaled that he was now his own man: "Lieberman Choice Sets Gore Apart from History, Clinton." George W. Bush's pick was just the opposite: "VP Pick Brings Up Father's Shadow" and "Safe but Dull Choice Fuses Dubya and Dad on Ticket." The *Washington Post* portrayed the Lieberman selection as "Integrity on the Ticket" but painted the selection of my dad as a perfunctory matter: "Bush Settles on Cheney for Ticket." The difference was so apparent that it caught the attention of Mark Shields, a Democrat and no fan of my Dad. "The press has been in Joe Lieberman's pocket," he observed one night on *The Capital Gang.* "I mean, let's be honest about it."

The Democrats had done their research and were quick to attack my dad and his record. Their strategy was to use a handful of votes from his years in Congress to undermine his image as a reasonable, thoughtful politician. If the Democrats were to be believed, Dad was a right-wing extremist who was in favor of plastic handguns and Nelson Mandela's imprisonment and opposed to the establishment of Martin Luther King, Jr.'s birthday as a federal holiday. We tried, of course, to explain why the Democrats weren't to be believed, but the press didn't find our explanations nearly as interesting as the charges.

Take the issue of plastic handguns, which had come up in the Congress twelve years before. The first thing to understand is that there was no such thing. All handguns contained metal parts. The 1988 bill banning plastic handguns was a PR stunt by the antigun lobby and its supporters on the Hill, and Dad, who has a low level of tolerance for PR stunts, voted against it. It was one of those votes that would have been pretty easy to take a dive on since it was basically a ban on something that didn't exist, and it certainly would have made life easier in 2000 if he had taken the easy way out—but, as we knew, that wasn't the way he had operated in Congress.

The Democrats had come up with another political ploy in 1986 with a nonbinding resolution calling for recognition of the African National Congress and the release of Nelson Mandela. Their idea—and Republicans have been known to have such ideas from time to time—was to get opponents on record voting for something they absolutely opposed, like recognition of the African National Congress, by pairing it with something they supported, like the release of Nelson Mandela. Dad wasn't about to endorse the ANC, which was believed to be a Marxist organization. Moreover, he thought it unconscionable for the bill's sponsors to use Nelson Mandela's imprisonment to try to extract a vote in favor of the ANC, particularly when the bill was a "nonbinding resolution" that would do absolutely nothing to get Mandela out of jail. Even though the House was controlled by the Democrats, many members agreed with my father, and the resolution failed to pass.

Dad had voted against establishing a federal holiday in honor of Martin Luther King, Jr.'s birthday in 1979, primarily because of the millions of dollars it costs to close the federal government for a holiday. But when the matter came up again in 1983, he listened carefully to the House debate, particularly to then congressman Jack Kemp, and changed his mind. Martin Luther King, Jr., and his vision of a just and tolerant America deserved commemoration, he decided, and he voted for a federal holiday honoring him.

We made our arguments to the press, they ignored us, and by the end of August, we were getting pretty tired of watching our poll numbers drop. When we got our campaign plane, the 727 that Governor Bush had been using, we were sure that by getting out on the road, we would reverse the slide. But it didn't work out that way. August 31, 2000, our first day on the road, was also day number one of the nine days of hell.

We were at Croissant Elementary School in Ft. Lauderdale, Florida, where Dad was to give a speech about No Child Left Behind, Governor Bush's proposal for improving our country's primary education system. A few days before the trip, however, the Clinton administration proposed a multimillion-dollar federal spending program to pay for new school construction, and the campaign staff back in Austin decided we needed a plan of our own. Unfortunately, there wasn't any room in Governor Bush's proposed budget to cover additional spending, so it was decided that the Bush-Cheney campaign would endorse the use of local bond initiatives to fund school construction—and that Dad would unveil the plan in his speech in Ft. Lauderdale.

Dad was wary of the idea from the start. He pointed out that local bond initiatives were just that, local. They weren't a federal issue and it didn't make a lot of sense to have national candidates talking about local bond issues. But he was the new kid on the block, the staff back in Austin had been thinking about these things longer than he had, and so he agreed to the plan.

On their arrival at Croissant Elementary, my parents took a quick tour, visited several classrooms, and posed for photos with the students. Everything was going really well, I thought—until I walked into the library and got my first look at the audience for the speech. I had assumed, and I'm sure Dad had assumed, that he'd be talking to school administrators, teachers, and parents. But the school library was full of kids, lots and lots of kids, basically the entire third and fourth grades.

I'd like to think that if it hadn't been so early in the campaign, if we'd had just a little more experience under our belts, we would have scrapped the speech and improvised. Mom could have read a book to the children and then Dad could have issued a statement to the media about the school bond issue. That's what we should have done, but instead, Dad walked up to the podium, pulled the speech out of his breast pocket, and delivered it as written. I was standing off to the side watching the kids listen to the speech. It was not a pleasant sight: Dozens of eight- and nine-year-olds were sitting cross-legged on the floor staring up at my dad with their mouths hanging open as he described the importance of school bond initiatives. It was painful to watch. I can't imagine what it was like for Dad to deliver that speech to that audience. He might as well have been speaking gibberish.

Afterward, he pulled me and Kathleen Shanahan aside and said, "No more school bond speeches." We both said, "Yes, sir," and Kathleen passed the message back to senior staff in Austin. But nobody there was pushing for another school bond speech. They were too busy wrestling with other matters.

One was the debates. The Commission on Presidential Debates had proposed and the Gore campaign had accepted three presidential and one vice presidential debate. Governor Bush had agreed to debate, but he wasn't in a rush to accept the commission's specific recommendations and was taking a lot of heat from the Democrats, who accused him of trying to avoid debating the vice president. To counter this, he announced in early September that he would debate Al Gore on *Meet the Press* on September 12, *Larry King Live* on October 3, and in St. Louis, for a debate proposed by the commission, on October 17. He also proposed two vice presidential debates.

When Vice President Gore refused this offer, the Bush campaign pointed out that he had previously agreed to debate Governor Bush any time, any place, and accused him of not being a man of his word. But the Democrats ignored that charge and began whaling away at George W. Bush for being a neophyte who was afraid to debate. That was a more powerful story line, and we were beaten up with it day after day until on September 9, the Bush campaign abandoned attempts to impose its own debate schedule. On September 15, the governor finally agreed to the commission's proposals.

The debate about the debates—a losing debate for us—wasn't the only negative news story dogging us in that first full week of September. There was also the story of an open microphone and a private conversation between Governor Bush and my father on Labor Day, September 3, the traditional kickoff for the fall campaign. The governor and Dad were just outside Chicago in Naperville, Illinois, for a Labor Day parade, and all of the broadcast and cable news networks were there to cover it.

Right before the parade, Dad and the governor spoke to a rally of a few hundred supporters. I was standing in the crowd and thought the event looked great: red, white, and blue balloon towers, lots of hand-painted signs, gorgeous sunshine. Dad introduced Governor Bush, who made brief remarks and got resounding cheers. Then he and my dad waved at the crowd, walked off the stage, and started down the parade route. What none of us knew was that a media microphone had picked up a private exchange between them while they were waving from the stage. Pointing out a reporter in the crowd, the governor had leaned over and said,

"There's Adam Clymer—major-league asshole from the *New York Times*." Within a few minutes, all of the cable news channels were airing the footage over and over again and running commentary about the lack of civility in politics.

Those of us at the parade had a few more minutes of blissful ignorance. I was several yards behind my dad, who was walking along, waving at people, and having a generally good time, when my cell phone and everyone else's started ringing. When I heard the news, I knew I had to tell Dad—though very quietly, since I didn't want anyone riding on the media's flatbed truck to hear me. He took it all calmly, just shook his head and wanted to know how the campaign was handling it.

I remember thinking how lucky we were that Dad hadn't said anything in response to the governor's comments—at least I thought he hadn't said anything. But within a few hours, one of the networks enhanced the audio on the tape, and every media outlet was reporting Dad's response to the governor's description of the *New York Times* reporter: "big-time." And I knew it was true. I'd heard him use that phrase countless times over the years.

The campaign tried to dismiss the comments by explaining that Dad and the governor were talking privately. They were sorry the candidates had been overheard, but they didn't apologize for the comments. That didn't satisfy reporters, but it wouldn't have mattered what we said. The press wasn't about to let this story go.

In the meantime, we had more campaigning to do. We split off from the governor, who was going to Michigan, and we stayed in the Chicago area and dropped by the Taste of Polonia Street Festival, a popular campaign stop for politicians of both parties. We were scheduled to do a quick in and out. Dad would make a few remarks, visit a couple of booths, and then we'd leave.

When we arrived at the street fair, Judy Topinka, the Illinois state treasurer and the Bush-Cheney point person for the event, pulled me aside to say that she thought it would be a great idea for my dad to dance a polka. She assured me that the crowd would love it. It was the last thing I could imagine my father doing, and I vetoed the idea. She then appealed to him, and he said that he didn't think it was a good idea either. I thought that killed the matter, but after he had made a few remarks to the crowd, Judy Topinka commandeered the microphone and announced, "Secretary Cheney will now dance a polka with Miss Polonia." Dad had no choice. He had to polka. So he grabbed Miss Polonia and away they went. She was nearly six feet tall, probably eighteen years old, and I think not overly thrilled about dancing with my father. But after a few turns, they got pretty good. Still, I knew this was not the picture we wanted on the evening news. But I also knew I didn't have to worry about it. There would be nothing from the Bush-Cheney campaign on the news that night except Governor Bush's description of the *New York Times* reporter and Dad's enthusiastic seconding of it.

As bad as Labor Day was, however, it was not our worst day on the campaign trail. That honor goes to Black Friday, September 8, 2000. On that day, three separate, unexpected, major news stories about my dad broke, a personal, if not a world, record.

It was supposed to be a relatively easy day for Dad: fly to Connecticut, give a speech on Governor Bush's plan for adding a prescription drug benefit to Medicare, attend a fundraiser, and then fly back to Washington, D.C., for a weekend of debate prep. But, as soon as I saw the early morning news clips, I knew we were in trouble. The *Dallas Morning News* was running a story claiming that Dad hadn't voted in fourteen of the sixteen elections that took place while he was living in Dallas, including the 2000 presidential primary.

Now, my dad has lived most of his life in Wyoming, a state

where people go to the polls every two years to vote on everything from city council and local bond issues to elections for state and federal officeholders. Texas is different. The state holds elections every two years, but individual jurisdictions can hold elections at other, seemingly random, times. Frequently, they are about a single local issue, aren't well publicized, and tend to draw only those voters with a strong interest in the outcome. The elections Dad missed included one for a local school board, two city elections, and a vote on school bonds (kind of ironic, given the speech in Florida). When we reviewed his travel schedule, we saw that many of these votes had taken place when he was out of town, and while he could have requested an absentee ballot, in most cases, he had not even been aware that an election had been scheduled.

The missed vote that drew most of the media attention was the Texas presidential primary in March 2000. Several reporters asked if it was appropriate for my dad to be Governor Bush's running mate if he hadn't bothered to vote in the presidential primary. Given that John McCain had dropped out of the presidential race before the Texas primary, that Governor Bush had already locked up the nomination by then, and that Dad had voted in the Wyoming primary, it seemed like it should have been a minor issue, but it wasn't. The traveling press corps hammered away on it until our plane touched down in Connecticut, at which point they switched over to the second story of the day.

As soon as we landed, we learned that Mark Nielsen, the Republican candidate for Connecticut's Fifth Congressional District, where my dad was campaigning, had just unveiled a new campaign ad. Underneath a banner reading "Leaders of Honor and Integrity" were photos of former president George H. W. Bush, Senator John McCain—and Senator Joe Lieberman. The Nielsen campaign claimed that it was sheer coincidence that the ad started running on the day that Dad arrived in the district, but I found it a little difficult to believe. They knew that having Dad in town would give them lots of free coverage for their stunt.

Our primary event of the day was pretty much a disaster. The motorcade took longer than expected, and we arrived late at an assisted living center where Dad was to give a speech on Medicare. My dad hates being late, so as we rushed into the event, none of us noticed that the room was inordinately warm. The advance men, apparently thinking we were going to arrive any minute, had turned off the noisy air-conditioning system a full hour before we arrived, and the temperature in the room was at least ninety degrees. Since Dad was now on stage speaking, we couldn't turn the air-conditioning back on because the noise would drown him out. The result was that most of the audience slept right through everything he had to say.

We'd set up several quick interviews for after the speech with local TV stations and newspapers so that Dad could reinforce his message about the importance of providing prescription drug coverage to seniors, but reporters didn't want to know about that. They wanted to ask about Mark Nielsen's ad. They were salivating at the prospect of some Republican infighting and kept pressing Dad. He wisely chose not to engage. "He can mention anybody he wants in his ads," he said. "He ought to run his own campaign so he wins in Connecticut." I have to admit that I checked on Election Day to see what happened to Mark Nielsen and took a certain satisfaction in the fact that he lost by twenty thousand votes.

The third news story broke when we were on our way to the fundraiser. Dirk Vandebeek, the press secretary traveling with my dad, said to me and Kathleen Shanahan, "AP is asking about a discriminatory toilet policy that was in place while Secretary Cheney was at Halliburton. Have you heard anything about it?" We hadn't and thought it sounded totally bizarre, but we spent the duration of the motorcade trying to track down the details.

It turns out that while operating in some foreign countries, Halliburton would have two sets of bathroom facilities: one for the locals and one for employees and contractors from the United States. There was nothing discriminatory about the policy. The two groups were used to using different types of toilets, and the company was trying to accommodate those differences. So we had a good answer for press inquiries, but decided it was best not to use it, not to say anything, and to refer the AP reporter directly to Halliburton. With everything else that was going on, the last thing the campaign needed to do was get involved in a debate over toilet policy. Since I was the personal aide, and the daughter, I was nominated to tell my dad about the story. The fundraiser he was headed for was closed to the press, but since the story was on the wires, he needed to know about it.

More than anyone else on the plane, Dad kept a positive attitude throughout what was an incredibly difficult and frustrating day. It takes a lot to get him to lose his temper, and he'd been calm and confident through all of the media's endless questions about the missed votes and the Nielsen ad, and he even managed to pivot back to the real issue of the day: reforming Medicare. When I told him about the press's latest line of inquiry, however, there was an expletive-deleted moment, then a disbelieving question: "They want to know about Halliburton's *toilet* policy?"

As I reflect back on that worst of all bad days, I think we were probably lucky that all three stories broke at the same time. Since they were competing with each other for headlines, none of them managed to get much traction and all were largely forgotten by the following week. I sure didn't feel lucky at the time, though. I spent most of the flight back to D.C. thinking that if this is what it was going to be like, it was going to be a long two months until the election.

As it turned out, the rest of September was a little better than the nine days of hell. Almost anything would have been. But it wasn't until early October, and my dad's debate with Joe Lieberman, that we really began to hit our stride.

CHAPTER 6

Expecting the Unexpected

Responding to a question about the increasingly partisan and personal nature of politics, Senator Lieberman reached into the breast pocket of his suit jacket, pulled out a piece of paper, and said, "I hope Secretary Cheney will join with me, right here on this stage tonight, in signing this pledge—a promise to raise the level of debate in this campaign, to focus on the issues, and to immediately stop running any and all inflammatory attack ads, which I fear have come to play an all-too-powerful role in our political process. So, how about it, Dick? Don't the American people deserve to hear about the issues in this election rather than just listening to an endless stream of personal attacks?"

My father took the piece of paper, turned toward the audience, and said, "Wait a minute. Does anyone really think he'll try something like that?"

We were in my parents' home in Jackson, Wyoming, and my dad was in the middle of a practice session for the 2000 vice presidential debate. According to the debate rules, candidates weren't supposed to use props or ask each other direct questions, but Ohio congressman Rob Portman, who was playing Senator Lieberman, had just done both. Portman's point—one strongly supported by political strategist Stuart Stevens, who was playing the moderator—was that just because something the rules say isn't allowed doesn't mean it won't happen. My dad had to be prepared for every possibility, including the possibility that his opponent might violate the rules.

Everyone agreed that if Senator Lieberman tried some out-of-bounds stunt during the debate, under no circumstances should Dad appeal to the moderator, or even point out that Senator Lieberman was violating the rules. It might be tempting, but it would look weak and whiny. The group in my parents' living room also agreed that it would be best if Dad didn't pick up the piece of paper or take the bait about the pledge. He should just ignore it and answer the moderator's question, focusing his response on George Bush's record as governor and talking about how often he had reached across the aisle to work with the Democrats in the Texas legislature.

The discussion reinforced an important lesson about debates and debate preps. It's not enough for the candidate to know all the details of every policy and to be comfortable with the talking points and his surroundings. He also has to expect, and deal with, the unexpected.

Every four years, some of the smartest, most respected deal-makers in politics, men like Jim Baker and Vernon Jordan, spend hours and hours negotiating a memorandum of understanding for the presidential and vice presidential debates. It covers every possible rule regarding how the candidates should act, from whether they may take notes and what kinds of pens they can use to whether they can ask each other questions and use props. But even after the agreement is signed there is no guarantee that the candidates will actually abide by it.

In 2000, the third presidential debate was a town hall meeting in which prescreened audience members asked questions of Vice President Gore and Governor Bush. During the debate, Vice President Gore interrupted Governor Bush while he was answering questions, tried to ask the governor several questions himself, and, at one point, even stalked across the stage into the governor's space in what can only be described as a menacing manner—all in violation of the memorandum of understanding worked out between the two campaigns. Governor Bush handled the situation extremely well. He kept his cool, looked at Al Gore, and nodded in a way that perfectly indicated how weird the vice president was being, and then he continued with his answer, ignoring the hulking man standing beside him. It was exactly the right thing to do.

It was also a situation that the governor had prepared for. Rob Portman had played Vice President Gore during a few of Governor Bush's prep sessions, and during one of their final run-throughs, he walked toward the governor and stood over him, trying to intimidate and distract him, but it didn't work. The governor reached up, grabbed him, and kissed him on the top of his head. It wasn't quite the response Governor Bush used on the real Al Gore, but the interchange gave him and his staff the opportunity to think about how to handle such a situation before it happened in a real debate.

While memoranda of understanding may not guarantee a candidate's good behavior, they are critical to establishing the format of the debates, which can range from a town hall meeting where candidates answer questions from audience members to a session where a single moderator puts queries to candidates seated at a table. Each side tries to negotiate the setting it thinks will be most advantageous for its candidate, which in our case was the seated, single-moderator format. My dad's team believed that format, sort of like a Sunday morning talk show, played to his strength, which is that he is deeply knowledgeable and thoughtful. Wandering around a stage and emoting, as some debate formats encourage, is not what he's best at. We were pleased that we ended up with what we called the *Meet the Press* format, and as it turned out, the seated debate played to Senator Lieberman's strength as well and allowed the two of them to have a thoughtful, substantive discussion of the issues of the day.

Agreeing to terms and formats, however, is only the first step in getting ready for a debate. The candidates spend countless hours studying briefing books, reviewing videotapes, and conducting practice sessions. The sheer amount of information the campaign staff generates is mind-boggling: policy books that outline every detail of every program each candidate has proposed; opposition books that include every public statement the opposing candidate has ever made, every vote that he has cast, every article that he has written, and an analysis of his debating style. And there are shelves full of videotapes of all of the opposing candidate's previous debates, television interviews, and in-depth profiles.

All of this information is distilled down to one or two binders for the candidate to study whenever he has time and that he can use for reference during his practice sessions. My dad's debate book was divided by issue, and under each one it gave anecdotes that could help put a personal face on the matter, key talking points, issue-specific attacks that could be used on the opposition, attacks that the opposition might use on my dad or on George W. Bush, and suggested responses to those attacks. For example, the section on education included:

- Recommendations to talk about some of the great teachers Dad had when he was growing up, like his third-grade teacher, Ms. Duffield, and Mr. Weishaar, a high school coach and math teacher.
- Facts about George Bush's record as governor of Texas, such as studies that showed that Texas students ranked first in the country in achievement, and its teachers ranked first in quality.
- Talking points emphasizing that improving public education is the most important challenge facing America today, that Governor Bush's education plan would increase school accountability, increase local control, and allow parents of disadvantaged children to move their child to a better school.
- Talking points regarding the Clinton-Gore administration's failure to close the achievement gap, including the fact that eight years after they had promised to improve our public schools, 68 percent of disadvantaged fourth-graders couldn't read.
- Points where Joe Lieberman's record on education conflicted with Al Gore's positions, such as his cosponsorship of Education Savings Accounts legislation that was later vetoed by the Clinton-Gore administration.
- Counters to possible pushbacks from Senator Lieberman. If the senator charged that Governor Bush's plan would siphon money from public education, one suggested response was for Dad to point out that competition will make public schools better and more accountable—which is, after all, the objective.

Pulling all of this material together required an incredible amount of effort and involved dozens of people, including researchers at the Republican National Committee, policy experts from the campaign, and teams of advisors who helped the candidates craft and practice their responses. To oversee this operation, every candidate needs someone who is smart, organized, pays attention to detail, can think strategically, and understands how to frame the best possible response to any question. That's where my sister, Liz, came in.

Liz managed Dad's debate prep and did an amazing job. She was responsible not just for his briefing materials, but also for planning and overseeing his practice sessions and running the post-practice debriefs, which were held after each practice session—and after my dad left the room. We decided that he had enough on his mind without having to sift through a dozen people's different opinions on how he could do better. That was Liz's job. She'd give everyone a chance to express his or her opinion, and then she would turn it all into a few key points to discuss with Dad. It wasn't always easy. One person might want Dad to aggressively go after Al Gore's plan for Medicare. Someone else might think he needed to spend more time explaining and defending Governor Bush's tax policy. And a third person might think that his answer on Bosnia needed to include more historical background on ethnic conflict in the Balkans. Somehow Liz would distill all this advice so it was helpful for Dad while making everyone in the room feel that they had made a substantial and important contribution to the process—which, indeed, they had.

Dad's practice sessions in 2000 always followed the same formula: There would be sixty or ninety minutes of mock debate, usually without interruption, then Dad would leave the room, and Liz would run the debrief.

My dad's debate prep sessions are the only ones I've ever attended, but from what I've read and heard, sessions vary widely depending on the candidate's style and the preparation he or she needs for the debate. Some candidates, like Vice President Gore, build sets that are exact duplicates of the debate hall, right down to the camera positions and the color of the carpet. The idea is to make the candidate comfortable and familiar with his surroundings before he ever sets foot onstage. In 2000, Senator Lieberman didn't go quite that far, but his debate team did use a table and chairs that were exactly like the ones that would be used in the debate. John Edwards supposedly had two replicas built in 2004, one in his house in Georgetown and the other in Chautauqua, New York, where he was cloistered for several days right before the debate.

My dad's attitude toward décor was much less demanding. In 2000, thinking it would be good practice to use an actual stage, we held a session at the Jackson Hole Playhouse, but the overstuffed red velvet chairs, the bar stools made out of old saddles, and the leafy stage decorations left over from a performance of *Seven Brides for Seven Brothers* didn't do much to elevate the proceedings, and after Liz found two reporters wandering through the theater acting like lost tourists just a few hours before we were scheduled to hold another session, we moved the rest of the sessions to my parents' house. It was easier and much more secure. We set up in the living room and used a couple of chairs out of the study and a rented folding table with a sheet thrown over it as our set. It was simple, and it let my dad focus on what he wanted to: learning what to expect from his opponent and developing his arguments.

Before each session, Dad spent hours reviewing his briefing book, reading through any updates that Liz had given him, and, most important, thinking about how he wanted to handle various questions and issues. Even though a candidate's briefing book always contains talking points or suggested answers, the best responses are usually the ones that the candidate creates for himself—at least that was the case with my dad. He'd read through all of his briefing materials, listen to feedback, and then construct his own answers. That way, they sounded like my dad, not like some preapproved set of talking points, and it also more accurately represented his point of view on the issue being discussed.

Dad and Liz intentionally kept the group for debate prep sessions small because, at some point, adding more people becomes counterproductive. While adding more people means more ideas and more points of view, it also increases the likelihood of conflict and competing agendas, and makes it that much harder for the group to give the candidate coherent and constructive advice. That's why we were all a little shocked when we heard that Vice President Gore had invited about a dozen "regular Americans" to travel to Florida to help out with his debate prep. None of us could imagine adding that many more people to my dad's sessions. It would have been like adding a focus group to the process and would have been completely chaotic and unhelpful. Given Vice President Gore's performance in the presidential debates, it didn't seem to have helped him very much either.

Our debate prep team was small, but it was outstanding. Rob Portman played Senator Lieberman, and it was a little eerie to watch him when he was in character. It was almost as if he was possessed by Joe Lieberman. He had spent countless hours watching videotapes of the senator's previous debates and interviews. He even had audiocassettes made of some of Senator Lieberman's speeches and would listen to them on his Walkman as he flew between Washington, D.C., his home in Ohio, and our practice sessions in Jackson. Not only did he master Senator Lieberman's speaking and debating styles, he had his mannerisms and hand gestures down pat. He was amazing to watch.

The rest of the Cheney 2000 debate prep team consisted of our family, a few key campaign staffers—particularly Kathleen Shanahan—and a trio of close friends and advisors from my dad's time as secretary of defense: Scooter Libby, Paul Wolfowitz, and Steve Hadley.

Without a doubt, my dad's best and most valued advisor was my mom. She's a great writer, can grasp an argument immediately, and she knows my dad better than anyone else. She is also better than anyone at putting a response into language that sounds like my dad. Maybe it's because they've been married for forty years, or because they've known each other since they were thirteen, but it's almost like they're joined at the cerebral cortex. Without even looking at each other, they can tell you exactly what the other one is thinking.

The other important player in any debate prep session is the moderator, because he can have a big impact on the tone of the debate, and on its outcome. In 1988, Bernard Shaw opened the second presidential debate by asking Michael Dukakis, "Governor, if Kitty Dukakis were raped and murdered, would you favor an irrevocable death penalty for the killer?" The graphic personal nature of the question shocked a lot of people in the audience, but Governor Dukakis's completely unemotional response was even worse. He talked about how the death penalty was not an effective way to deal with violent crime. It was the one truly memorable moment of that debate, and it was triggered by the moderator.

Bernard Shaw also moderated the vice presidential debate in 2000, and political strategist Stuart Stevens and my brother-in-law Phil Perry took turns playing him during Dad's prep sessions. Stuart in particular seemed to take special joy in coming up with Shaw-style questions designed to get an emotional response from my dad, such as, "Secretary Cheney, the Bush campaign seemed to have been surprised by a number of disclosures about your background—past votes as a congressman, stock options from Halliburton. You were in charge of the vetting process for other potential candidates. Who, sir, vetted you?"

As always, Dad decided that the best way to answer such questions was to be honest and direct. If Bernie Shaw asked about his voting record, Dad would point out that he cast thousands of votes while he was in Congress, and, as often happens in political campaigns, his opponents had chosen to take a small handful of those votes out of context. As for the stock options from Halliburton, Dad's answer was that, if elected, he would donate all of his unvested options to charity. Stuart Stevens's goal in asking these questions wasn't to try to stump or surprise my dad, it was to give him the opportunity to think about how to respond to a question presented this way—to help him expect the unexpected.

We didn't know whether Bernie Shaw would ask about gay rights, but a question on gay marriage did come up in a practice session. My dad's response was that it was a matter for the states to decide. It wasn't a memorable answer, but I think the consensus was that when an issue causes strong feelings, as gay rights does, bland is probably all right. It's a measure of how much my dad thinks about things, turning them over in his mind that, when Bernie Shaw did ask a gay rights question, my dad gave an answer that is still quoted today.

Shaw asked whether gays and lesbians should have "all the constitutional rights enjoyed by every American citizen." My dad said:

> The fact of the matter is we live in a free society and
> freedom means freedom for everybody. We shouldn't be
> able to choose and say you get to live free and you don't.
> That means that people should be free to enter into any
> kind of relationship they want to enter into. It's no one's
> business in terms of regulation of behavior in that regard.
> The next step then, of course, is the question you ask of
> whether or not there ought to be some kind of official
> sanction of the relationships or if they should be treated

the same as a traditional marriage. That's a tougher problem. That's not a slam dunk. The fact of the matter is that matter is regulated by the states. I think states are likely to come to different conclusions, and that's appropriate. I don't think there should necessarily be a federal policy in this area. I try to be open-minded about it as much as I can and tolerant of those relationships. And like Joe, I'm wrestling with the extent to which there ought to be legal sanction of those relationships. I think we ought to do everything we can to tolerate and accommodate whatever kind of relationships people want to enter into.

It was a terrific answer, but more important, it didn't come from the talking points or from some political spin. It came from my dad. It was what he thought and felt and believed.

The most difficult responses to come up with are the humorous ones, the funny, biting one-liners that can define an entire ninety-minute debate. Done correctly, they're the most effective way for a candidate to draw attention to an opponent's shortcomings or to counter a perceived weakness of his own. During the 1984 Democratic primaries, Walter Mondale criticized the lack of substance in some of Gary Hart's policy proposals by saying, "Where's the beef?" Later that year, Ronald Reagan dismissed critics who suggested he was too old to continue serving as president by announcing during a debate, "I will not make age an issue in this campaign. I'm not going to exploit for political purposes my opponent's youth and inexperience." In 1988, Lloyd Bentsen uttered what may be the most famous and devastating line in debate history when he told Dan Quayle, "Senator, I served with Jack Kennedy. I knew Jack Kennedy. Jack Kennedy was a friend of mine. Senator, you're no Jack Kennedy."

Part of the reason all those lines worked so well was that each of them fit perfectly with a specific question from the moderator or with a statement made by the candidate's opponent. In Senator Bentsen's case, Senator Quayle had just said that he had as much experience as John F. Kennedy had when he was elected president. The Senator from Indiana had gotten in the habit of using that line out on the campaign trail to counter the charge that he wasn't ready to be president, and Senator Bentsen, knowing there was a good chance that he would use it in their debate, crafted an unforgettable response. Usually, however, the targets aren't so clear or predictable, and it's incredibly difficult to prepare one-liners ahead of time.

During our practice sessions, people would periodically come up with a line that they thought might be a good comeback or a funny response for my dad to use; a few longtime friends even emailed or faxed us their lists of suggested lines. Unfortunately, most of them really weren't that funny, and more than a few were what I would call groaners—the response I expected from the audience if Dad actually used them during the debate. Suggested lines included:

- References to popular culture—"Well Joe, if you'd been at the Olympics in Sydney, you would have won a gold medal in exaggeration on that one," or, "On Election Day, the American people are going to vote Al Gore off the island."
- References to the controversy over Al Gore's dog's arthritis medication—"Looks like Al Gore's dog ate his prescription drug plan."
- References to my dad's love of fishing—"I know a thing or two about fishing—and that sure sounds like a fish story to me."

In the end, the funniest exchange of the debate was the result of my dad taking advantage of remarks by Senator Lieberman:

Lieberman: I think if you asked most people in America today that famous question that Ronald Reagan asked, "Are you better off today than you were eight years ago?" most people would say yes. I'm pleased to see, Dick, from the newspapers that you're better off than you were eight years ago, too. (Laughter from the audience)

Cheney: I can tell you, Joe, the government had absolutely nothing to do with it. (Laughter and applause from the audience)

Shaw: This question to you . . .

Lieberman (interrupting): I can see my wife and I think she's saying, "I think he should go out into the private sector."

Cheney: Well, I'm going to try to help you do that, Joe. (Laughter, applause, and cheering from the audience)

I was stunned when Senator Lieberman interrupted Bernie Shaw to make his comment about going into the private sector—I couldn't believe that he would give my dad such an opening—and it was great to watch Dad take full advantage of it. His response was perfect.

There were several reasons Dad did so well, but one of the most important was that he took time to relax and rest up. He and my mom decided to stay at their house in McLean, Virginia, the night before the debate, so he could get a good night's sleep, even though it meant an hour-and-a-half flight and an hour-long motorcade to the debate site in Danville, Kentucky. He also, very wisely, turned down requests from the staff in Austin to do several high-profile public events the day of the debate, and he resisted any suggestion of squeezing in one last practice session. The last thing any candidate wants to do is walk onstage tired or overprepared. He or she needs to be confident, comfortable, and relaxed. The only public event Dad did before the debate was a small welcome rally with a few hundred supporters in Lexington, Kentucky. After that, it was on to Danville for the walk-through and some downtime.

The walk-through was the first time we saw the auditorium, and it was completely different from either the Jackson Playhouse or my parents' living room. The stage seemed huge, multileveled with bright red carpeting. We all took turns trying out the chairs for Dad and Bernie Shaw, while my three-year-old niece, Elizabeth, claimed the one for Senator Lieberman. She found a ballpoint pen and began earnestly decorating the senator's name tag. When we asked her what she was drawing, she said, "a dinosaur," and kept right on with her task. We thought Senator Lieberman would appreciate her drawing. It was a really good-looking dinosaur. But the staff of the Commission on Presidential Debates disagreed and had the name tag reprinted before the Liebermans arrived.

After our walk-through, we went to a historically correct bed-and-breakfast in Danville for several hours of downtime. It had a lot of charm, but not much in the way of air-conditioning, so Dad commandeered the one room in the back that was semicool and took a nap. The rest of us were too nervous and excited to relax, so my mom took the grandkids outside to play while Liz and I tried to find some news on the one television set we could find. We tuned in to *Inside Politics* on CNN just as they announced the latest CNN/Gallup tracking numbers. The three-day tracking poll showed Al Gore leading George Bush by eleven points (51–40). Liz and I discussed whether to tell Dad the numbers. Most polls showed Vice President Gore with a slight lead, but nothing this dramatic. It had to be wrong, and telling Dad right before his debate couldn't possibly do any good, so we decided not to mention it to him until after the debate was over.

For me, the most stressful time of the whole day was waiting to go to the hall. It felt like the afternoon that wouldn't end. Everything was set for the debate and the postdebate rally, and the spin operation was in place. There wasn't anything that any of us could do but wait. Some of the staff watched TV in the hold room. Others tried to catch up on sleep. I managed to kill an hour or so by going for a long walk. I'm not sure about anyone else, but I was relieved when it was finally time to go to Danville's Centre College for what local people were calling "The Thrill in the Ville."

Dad's hold room was a small, dark, low-ceilinged room backstage. To help brighten it up, the advance team had appropriated every floor and desk lamp that they could find. Since there wasn't enough counter space, there were lamps all over the floor, so you had to watch where you were stepping or you risked tripping over a cord or kicking over a lamp.

We deliberately kept the number of people in the room to the absolute minimum. Dad didn't want to be distracted or to have to listen to any last-minute advice. Mom was with him, Liz and I went in to wish him luck and to tell him how proud we were of him, and a few close friends like Scooter Libby and Paul Wolfowitz stopped by for a quick hello, but that was really it. Everyone else was either in their seats in the auditorium or in the spin room waiting for the debate to start.

When I read the book that Senator Lieberman and his wife, Hadassah, wrote about the campaign, I was struck by the description of their hold room. It was full of people—family, friends, and advisors—and when Senator Lieberman was getting ready to go onstage, they all held hands and sang the song, "This Little Light of Mine." I can completely imagine Senator Lieberman doing that, but it's just about the last thing that my dad, or the rest of us, would do before a debate, or any other time. I guess you could say that we're more buttoned-down. What we did do was give Dad a card of reminders that Liz had prepared for him to take with him. Items on the card included:

- "Glad to be here and glad to talk about it"—Sometimes candidates come across as annoyed or bothered when they have to debate. It was important to come across as happy and grateful to have the opportunity to discuss these important issues in front of the American people.
- "Education Education Education"—Whenever possible, talk about education and the fact that a Bush-Cheney administration would take steps to improve our public education system.
- "Reformer with results"—Whenever possible, talk about George Bush's record of accomplishment as governor of Texas.

But even our most buttoned-down of families had something else we wanted him to think about. So Liz had written a message from all of us at the bottom of the card: "Remember that your wife, your daughters, and your granddaughters are all incredibly proud of you and love you very much."

I was a little nervous before the debate, but once it got started, I was fine. Dad looked great—comfortable, confident, relaxed. He wore a dark blue shirt, unusual for a presidential or vice presidential debate, but for my dad, who can seem pretty formal and intimidating, it was a softening touch. His answers on defense and foreign policy issues demonstrated the depth of his knowledge and experience, and his responses on domestic and social issues were thoughtful and serious. When Bernie Shaw asked both candidates to imagine that they were African-American and had become the target of racial profiling and to discuss what they would do, my dad began his answer this way:

Bernie, I'd like to answer your question to the best of
my ability, but I don't think I can understand fully what
it would be like. I try hard to put myself in that position
and imagine what it would be like, but of course, I've
always been part of the majority, never been part of a
minority group. But it has to be a horrible experience,
the anger, frustration, and rage that would go with
knowing that the only reason you were stopped, the
only reason you were arrested, was because of the color
of your skin.

He went on to say that despite the enormous progress we have
made in race relations in this country, we still have a long way to go.
Racial profiling is one example, but we also have to close the
achievement gap in education and address income differentials
and differences in lifespan. We are still a society, he said, that hasn't
done enough to live up to the ideal that Martin Luther King articu-
lated of judging people by the content of their character and not
the color of their skin.

When Bernie Shaw announced that it was time for closing
statements, it didn't seem possible that ninety minutes had gone
by. Dad had done an incredible job, and we all got up from our
seats and engaged in the final contest of every political debate—the
race onstage to congratulate the candidate. It was close, but I'm
pretty sure our family won by at least a couple of seconds.

Looking back on it, Dad's performance in the vice presidential
debate was one of the high points of the 2000 campaign. After suf-
fering through almost two months of negative news stories and
bad poll numbers, he finally had the opportunity to show why
George W. Bush had chosen him to be his running mate, and he
came through with flying colors. It was a substantive and intelli-

gent exchange on both sides, and while the Democrats tried to spin it as a tie, we all knew that Dad won hands down.

Our whole family was riding high after the debate. We had a great late-night victory rally with a few thousand enthusiastic supporters packed into a local school gym, and then we stayed up into the early hours of the next day watching replays of the debate on C-SPAN. There was still another month before the election, but we were energized, optimistic, and ready to go.

CHAPTER 7

Life on the Road

Before I ever worked on a presidential campaign, I'd heard former staffers tell tales of adventure and hard work on the campaign trail. They'd talk about flying around the country, fighting for every vote, and making a difference. Sometimes they would explain how they had single-handedly snatched electoral victory from the jaws of certain defeat. It all sounded incredibly exciting, demanding, and adventurous, but then no one ever mentioned the bedbugs. Being on the road during a presidential campaign is an amazing experience, but it is definitely not a glamorous or luxurious life.

Every dollar a campaign spends on travel is a dollar it doesn't get to spend on advertising, polling, or getting out the vote. So campaigns try to stretch the travel budget as far as humanly possible, and as a result, candidates and their staffs frequently stay in some pretty bad hotels. During the 2000 campaign, there were times when it seemed that the staff back in Austin was maybe a little too good at finding the most economical hotel rooms.

One night, the rooms were not only bad, but there weren't enough of them, so I ended up sleeping on an old, very lumpy roll-away bed set up in the living room of my parents' suite. I fell asleep as soon as my head hit the pillow, and it wasn't until my alarm went off the next morning that I realized something was wrong, very wrong—from the neck down I was covered with huge, itchy welts—bedbug bites. I spent the next several days applying ice packs, dousing myself in calamine lotion and popping Benadryl tablets, anything that might give me some relief.

One hotel had pale, pastel green sheets on all of its beds. They looked institutional, but I didn't think much of it until I pulled back the covers and saw the stamps claiming the sheets as property of one of the local county hospitals. I told myself that the hotel must have bought an overrun of sheets made for the hospital, which was definitely a more comforting explanation than the alternative—that the hotel had bought them secondhand.

In another hotel, the bed in my parents' room was a creaky, saggy, thirty-year-old Murphy bed that folded out of the wall. When they pulled it down, they discovered that at any given moment only one of the bed's legs touched the ground. The problem was that it wasn't always the same leg. Any movement, such as breathing, would rock the bed, forcing the leg that was on the ground to rise and the leg that was in the air to land on the floor with a loud "thunk." After discovering this delightful feature, my parents decided that it was my duty as the personal aide, and more important as their daughter, to swap rooms with them. I didn't really have much choice in the matter, so I curled up on one corner of the Murphy bed and tried to remain perfectly still while I fell asleep. It didn't work. Breathing wasn't really an optional activity, so I relocated to the floor.

One of the worst nights of the 2000 campaign, however, would have to be the night we stayed in two different hotels. The first one was great. It was clean and had a friendly staff and an ice machine on every floor. It just didn't have any electricity. While my parents were at a fundraiser, the power went off, which, even in those pre-9/11 days, was a security concern. There were no thunderstorms to account for the loss of power, nor was anything beyond the hotel affected. When my parents returned, the Secret Service held them in the car in the hotel driveway while a couple of helicopters circled overhead, probing the area around the hotel with searchlights. After an hour or so, a decision was made to relocate to another hotel just down the street. It sounded easy enough, but my parents had been staying on the twelfth floor of a hotel that had no lights and no working elevators. Several staff members and I climbed the twelve flights, stumbled around in the dark until we found all of their luggage, and then carried everything all the way back down to the lobby. Fortunately, enough people were helping, so we had to make only one trip.

We could tell right away that the second hotel wasn't great, but by the time we got my parents checked in, everyone was too exhausted to care. My mom went right to sleep, but was awakened by snoring. She initially thought it was coming from my dad, but he was awake and reading. The snoring, it turned out, was coming from the gentleman next door. The walls were so thin that it sounded like he was in their room.

No matter how bad the hotel room is, unless it involves bedbugs, it somehow seems tolerable, probably because you know it's only for one night. Tomorrow means a new hotel, and at least the hope of a better room, perhaps even one that doesn't have red shag carpeting on the walls or a heart-shaped bathtub in the middle of the room. It also helps to remember that when you're on the road, your home isn't the hotel—that's just where you try to sleep for a few hours every night. On the road, your home is the plane.

When Governor Bush finally took custody of his new campaign

plane at the end of August, we got the old Bush-Cheney 727. It was well worn and had seen some heavy use, but at least it was ours. No more hopscotching around the country on small charter planes while the press corps tried to keep up on commercial flights. For the last two months of the campaign we would all be together on one plane, our home on the road.

My assigned seat was up near the front and faced backward. It was lumpy and wouldn't recline even an eighth of an inch, but I was just happy that we'd finally gotten the plane. After our first landing, however, I realized that I'd been assigned the seat of death. The plane was old enough that the luggage compartments tended to pop open, and since it was a charter, some FAA regulations were less strictly enforced than others, particularly those about securing all carry-on luggage and turning all trash and snack items over to the flight attendants before landing. The result was that whenever we touched down, there would be loud crashing noises as things from the back of the plane came flying forward: fruit, candy, drinking glasses, a briefing book that had popped out of an overhead, three or four cell phones. Sitting in a backward-facing seat was kind of like being the knife-thrower's assistant in a circus sideshow. Things would fly at me, but I was strapped in place and couldn't do a thing about it, except hope that they would miss. What is truly amazing is that it took me a week, and getting clocked by a bottle of water, before I decided to relocate to an unclaimed seat that faced forward.

After every landing, there would be a brief free-for-all as everyone gathered up their phones, pagers, purses, and other items that had broken free on landing. Since all the campaign cell phones were identical, there was no guarantee that the phone you retrieved was actually the one that was assigned to you, and this was a source of frequent confusion. After one particularly hard landing,

Emily Kertz, one of the communications staffers, couldn't find her phone. A couple of days later, Mom mentioned to me that she seemed to be getting a lot of wrong numbers on hers, and asked, "Why do people keep calling and asking for Emily?" It was then that I realized what had happened.

Without a doubt the worst landings were always in Jackson, Wyoming, where the altitude is high and the runway short. Whenever we were on final approach there, the staff took bets on whether we were going to go off the end of the runway. We never did, but we sure got close a few times. One of our airplane's few redeeming features was that it had really good brakes.

Takeoffs were generally less adventuresome than landings—except when we didn't take off. Toward the end of the 2000 campaign, we were about to board the plane in Portland, Maine, when we saw the pilot and crew coming down the stairs. There was some kind of billing dispute between the charter company and the campaign, and the charter company had decided that the best way to get the campaign's attention was to ground the crew. It was several hours before the staff back at campaign headquarters got matters worked out with the charter company and we could leave for our next destination.

One incident, however, single-handedly made up for all of our planes' failings. On one of the last flights of the campaign, Jay Parmer, the tour director who oversaw all of our travel plans, announced that there was a small problem: The lavatory system was oozing blue goo into one of the cargo holds. As it happened, it was the hold that contained the press corps' luggage. The goo didn't pose a danger to the plane or its passengers, but it did turn the contents of several reporters' suitcases a rather unappetizing shade of blue. After a campaign in which our relations with some of the reporters had grown a little strained, we tried really hard to seem sympathetic about the awful things the blue goo did to their luggage and their clothes, but it was tough not to find a little humor in the situation.

Our plane had issues, but basically we were safe. I'm not so sure that was true of a charter that my mom took while she was on a "W stands for Women" tour with Laura Bush, Condi Rice, and Cindy McCain. At the beginning of the campaign, Mom bought an inflatable neck pillow. Liz and I would give her a fair amount of grief about it whenever she blew it up and tucked it around her neck, but it did seem to help her sleep on planes. On the "W stands for Women" plane, however, the pillow behaved strangely. It started growing in size, getting firmer and firmer as the plane gained altitude. Thinking there might be a pressurization problem, my mom called a Secret Service agent over; he took one look at the pillow and headed for the cockpit. The crew assured him there was no problem, no problem at all—but just then oxygen masks started dropping from the ceiling. People tried breathing from them, but if there was any oxygen coming out, it wasn't enough. One of the agents fell ill, then Mrs. McCain, which was enough to convince everybody that it was time for an emergency landing, and the plane set down in Tulsa, Oklahoma, where the touring women waited for the campaign to dispatch another plane to pick them up.

Life on the road isn't all bad hotels and scary plane rides. It's also learning to wear a black suit to any occasion (they don't show wrinkles or dirt); being made happy by small things (like finding out that they will be serving something other than taco salad on the next flight); and training yourself to put a piece of paper next to your bed that lists your name, the date, the city you are in, and the departure time for the motorcade (in case you wake up in the middle of the night, and can't remember).

One thing that everyone on the road worries about is baggage call. Before the candidate and traveling staff arrive at a hotel for an overnight stay, the advance team tapes a piece of paper to the mirror in each hotel room letting everyone know the exact time they have to have their bags ready for pickup the next morning. If your bags aren't packed and outside your door by that time, you are responsible for getting them to the plane yourself, not an easy thing to do in a tightly packed motorcade. Because baggage call is usually very early (5:00 A.M. is not unusual), staffers quickly figure out how to organize their lives so that they can put their bags out before they go to bed.

In 2000, one staffer traveled all over the country carrying her pajamas in her laptop computer bag. Every night, she would pick out her clothes for the next day, change into her pajamas, repack her bags, and put them in the hall before she went to bed. When she got up the next morning, she simply carried her pajama-filled computer bag onto the plane. When I asked her about it, she pointed out that this system not only kept her from having to get up before baggage call, but it meant she was also prepared if her bags didn't show up at the next night's hotel. She could still put on her pajamas and go to bed. She'd just have to make sure the suit she took off was in good enough shape to wear again the following day—not a problem if the suit was black.

Putting your bags out early, however, is not without risk. One staffer kept forgetting to leave out shoes to wear the next day. Invariably by the time he realized his mistake, his bags would be gone and he'd show up for the motorcade in his bare feet. Once he got on the plane, he would have to beg the baggage handlers to unearth his suitcase so he could get his shoes for the day.

One of the greatest fears on the road is losing your luggage. Given how tight the travel schedule is, once it's lost, it's gone for good. It will never catch up with you. Toward the end of the 2000 campaign, one staffer (I'll call him Al) from Austin spent a week traveling with my dad. Unfortunately, the airline he flew to meet us lost all of his bags. There was no time to go shopping for new clothes, so Al had to wear the same suit for six days. On day five, Kathleen Shanahan, my dad's chief of staff, found him sitting by himself in the staff van, a fifteen-passenger van that travels at the end of the motorcade. According to the manifest, several other staffers should have been riding with him, so Kathleen asked where everyone was. Al hemmed and hawed, but finally explained that after five days in the same clothes, he'd become a little ripe, and the rest of the staff had gone off in search of better-smelling cars.

Everyone deals with the stresses of the road differently. Some people develop an almost fanatical dedication to exercise. They would rather work out than sleep and will go running at any hour of the day or night to get their five miles in. More common are the people who eat everything that is put in front of them regardless of whether they're hungry. It's part of the reason so many campaign staffers go on diets after an election. One staffer complained whenever we stayed in a nice hotel. She didn't mind the clean room, but she had developed a minibar problem. She wasn't drinking the minibottles of wine and liquor, but she was eating all of the snacks, and the $15.00 jars of macadamia nuts and the $4.50 bags of M&M's were starting to add up.

Some staffers spend their time on the road documenting the campaign trail. Generally, they take pictures of events, but some people develop more specialized tastes. One of the baggage guys traveling with Governor Bush took photos of all the mullets he saw on the road and became quite an expert on the different types and styles of the infamous short-in-front, long-in-back haircut. He could tell a Tennessee Top Hat from a Kentucky Waterfall at a single glance. Another took a picture of every car that he rode in. By the end of the campaign, he'd built up an impressive collection of photos of minivans from across the country.

One of the things you get used to on the road is repetition—events and speeches look and sound very similar day after day. Members of the traveling press corps complain about this, but even they understand that the way to get the campaign's message across is to repeat it again and again. It will be new to the people in the audience and the local media covering the event. As far as the campaign staff is concerned, when something new and unexpected happens, it's usually bad.

In October 2000, Dad was in Las Vegas to give a speech and to hold a roundtable with several local reporters. Nevada was shaping up as a key battleground state and we were doing everything we could to get our message out in the local press.

Dad knew that one of the issues that was bound to come up in his interviews was the proposed nuclear waste storage facility at Yucca Mountain—less than one hundred miles from Las Vegas. Reading through his briefing papers, he noticed that there wasn't much information on Yucca Mountain, just a very vague statement of the campaign's position: that Governor Bush was aware of the controversy regarding the storage of nuclear waste at Yucca Mountain and that he would base his decision on what the available scientific research recommended as the best and safest course of action.

Knowing that answer wouldn't satisfy the reporters, Dad called Kathleen Shanahan and the policy staffer who was traveling with us that week and asked them to see if they could get more information out of the policy shop in Austin. They tried, but the staff back in Austin didn't have anything new to add.

After the speech, Dad sat down at a small table with a group of local reporters. Al Simpson, the former senator from Wyoming and a close family friend who was traveling with my dad that week, sat down next to him. The roundtable went something like this:

Reporter 1: Secretary Cheney, do you and Governor Bush support the use of Yucca Mountain as a storage site for nuclear waste?

Dad (smiling): Governor Bush is aware of the controversy regarding the storage of nuclear waste at Yucca Mountain and he will base his decision on what the available scientific research recommends as the best and safest course of action.

Reporter 2: Secretary Cheney, does that mean that you and Governor Bush would move to store nuclear waste at Yucca Mountain, even though a majority of Nevadans are opposed to the project?

Dad (still smiling, but not quite as much): Governor Bush is aware of the controversy regarding the storage of nuclear waste at Yucca Mountain and he will base his decision on what the available scientific research recommends as the best and safest course of action.

Reporter 3: So do you support the storage of nuclear waste at Yucca Mountain?

Dad (not smiling at all): You know, I've got someone I'd like you all to meet, my new policy advisor. Maybe he can help shed some light on this issue for us.

At that point, Dad, the reporters, and Senator Simpson all turned toward the back of the room to the policy staffer, who seemed stunned and appalled to find himself the center of attention. He sat silently immobile for a few seconds, then jumped up and ran out of the room without uttering a single word. I remember turning to Juleanna Glover, the press secretary, and saying, "That can't possibly be a good sign."

In his defense, the policy staffer had gone to call back to headquarters in Austin to get some more information, but none of us knew that at the time, and before we could run after him, a new, more pressing situation arose. Senator Simpson is one of my all-time favorite people. He's smart, he's funny, and he will not hesitate to tell you exactly what he is thinking—even if it's not what you want to hear, or what is included in the preapproved talking points. After the policy staffer ran out of the room, Senator Simpson turned to the reporters and said, "Look—the nuclear waste has to go somewhere—it's going to come here—so you better just get used to it." It was a pretty clear statement—nowhere near the approved language that we had been given—and it pretty effectively and dramatically brought an end to the media roundtable.

As we headed toward the airport, every staffer with a cell phone was dialing madly, trying to figure out what to do. Kathleen Shanahan finally decided that the communications staff back in Austin should call all the reporters from the roundtable and try to put as much distance as possible between the campaign and Senator Simpson's remarks.

If Senator Simpson had been any other VIP, the staff wouldn't have worried about his feelings, but everyone on the plane really liked and respected him and none of us wanted him to know that the campaign was calling reporters to tell them that he wasn't speaking on behalf of the Bush-Cheney campaign. We decided that someone—meaning me—had to make sure that he didn't see any of the news clips from the Las Vegas event. Fortunately, the senator was on the plane for only one more day, because I think he got suspicious when I told him that all of the printers and fax machines on the plane had suddenly broken down and couldn't be repaired.

Some of the best stories about unexpected happenings on the campaign trail have nothing to do with policy. One of my favorites is about the tax-family events that were a part of almost every airport arrival in 2000. At each stop, there would be a local family, arranged for by the campaign, waiting for my dad when he got off the plane. Dad would introduce them to the local media and then explain in very specific terms how much better off the family would be under Governor Bush's tax plan than under Vice President Gore's.

The backdrop for each of the presentations was a giant 1040 form that we hauled around. Whenever we landed, one of the baggage guys, a really nice college kid I'll call Bill, would hustle it off the back of the plane and set it up on an easel so that Dad and the tax family could stand in front of it. It was simple, it was effective, and except for one incident in the Midwest, it was flawless.

Dad was scheduled to fly from St. Louis, Missouri, to Cedar Rapids, Iowa, for a small event with a group of senior citizens. As usual, the campaign had arranged for a tax family to meet the plane in Cedar Rapids. Unfortunately, thunderstorms kept us circling for over an hour in bad turbulence before we were finally diverted to Council Bluffs. Working quickly, the staff found a television studio so Dad could do a live satellite feed back to the event in Cedar Rapids. Everything was set, except no one had told Bill about the change in plans.

Like many campaign staffers, Bill had developed the ability to sleep through almost anything, and he made it through the thunderstorms and heart-stopping turbulence without ever opening an eye. He finally woke up when the plane came to a stop on the tarmac in Council Bluffs, and assuming we were in Cedar Rapids, he grabbed the giant 1040 form and ran off the back of the plane before anyone could stop him. Looking out the windows, we all watched as Bill frantically ran around the tarmac, carrying the giant form, looking for the tax family.

After a few minutes, Jay Parmer took pity on Bill and called him on the radio. All of us who had radios heard the following exchange:

Jay (calmly): Bill, this is Jay.
Bill (frantically): Where's tax family? I can't find the tax family.
Jay (still calm): The tax family is in Cedar Rapids.
Bill (still frantic): I know. I have to find them. Where did the advance team put them? Are they in the terminal?
Jay (trying not to laugh): The tax family is in Cedar Rapids. You are in Council Bluffs.
Bill (no longer running or frantic): Oh.

Once Bill realized his mistake, he sheepishly dragged the giant tax form back on the plane, and as he walked past the traveling press corps, they gave him a standing ovation—the only standing ovation our press corps ever gave anyone.

CHAPTER 8

Election Day

It was almost 2:00 A.M. on November 8, 2000, in Austin, Texas, and it was finally over. George W. Bush was going to be the next president of the United States, and my father was going to be the next vice president. We were on our way to the governor's mansion to meet with the Bush family, then all of us we were going to the big celebration on Congress Avenue. After three months of campaigning, and one very long night of watching returns, we were exhausted but thrilled. As we walked down to the motorcade, everyone was smiling, laughing, and celebrating—everyone, that is, except my dad.

Because the Secret Service prefers to take protectees through back entrances rather than the front door, the motorcade was lined up outside the service entrance of the Four Seasons Hotel. The only way to get to the service entrance was by following the agents on a long circuitous route down service elevators and back hallways. As we made our way through the hotel's kitchen, my mom leaned over to my dad and whispered, "You've just been elected vice president of the United States. You could at least look happy about it." Because of all the people around, Dad didn't say anything, just shook his head, but when we asked him about it later, he said it just hadn't felt right, that he had thought it was too early for the networks to be making the call. He'd been through the 1976 election when the race had been so close that President Ford hadn't conceded until the following day, and 2000 was proving to be an even tighter race. The networks had already made one mistake when they prematurely called Florida for Vice President Gore, and now Dad thought they might be making another by calling it for us too soon. It was a feeling that would prove to be eerily correct.

Election Day had started with my parents voting at the local firehouse in Jackson. We had all boarded the plane for Austin absolutely convinced that we were going to win. The last round of tracking polls had shown the race tightening, but almost all of the polls put Governor Bush up by two to three points. The only real question was how big the victory was going to be.

We wouldn't get any more numbers until the first exit polls came out in the early afternoon, so to help pass the time, we held a contest—guess the number of electoral votes that George W. Bush was going to win. Most people guessed between 300 and 350. I picked 329. A few staffers were feeling especially optimistic and guessed we'd win over 400 electoral votes, including California's 54. Kristienne Perry, my brother-in-law Phil's sister, a very smart person with absolutely no political experience, guessed low—272 electoral votes—enough for the governor to win, but barely. The rest of us teased her for being so pessimistic. Then we got the first exit poll numbers.

Voter News Service was responsible for conducting exit polls during the 2000 election. Founded in 1993 by a consortium of major news organizations including ABC, CBS, NBC, CNN, and Fox, VNS selected sample precincts and interviewed voters as they left their polling places. Voters were asked a wide range of questions regarding themselves, which candidates they voted for, and why they voted for them. The results were compiled and released to the news organizations, which then used them during their election-night coverage, particularly as they made their projections of the winner of each state. While the survey results were supposed to remain confidential until the polls closed in each state, campaign employees could usually get them from friends in the media.

We were about thirty minutes away from landing in Austin when Kathleen Shanahan, Dad's chief of staff, called back to headquarters and got the first exit poll numbers. They weren't good. They showed George W. Bush trailing in almost every battleground state including the big three: Pennsylvania, Michigan, and Florida. If these numbers were right, at best we were in for a long night. At worst, we would probably lose the election.

Liz and I were both pretty upset, Mom tried to put on a brave face, and Dad, being the most even-keeled person on the face of the earth, took the news in stride. He told us that early exit polls are frequently wrong, so we shouldn't get upset over one batch of bad numbers. He also told us that no matter how we felt, we had to look and act as though we were confident that we were going to win. The staff and the press would be watching us, and if we hung our heads or looked upset, the press would report it and the staff would take it as a sign that we'd given up. We had to stay positive and upbeat, particularly since the polls were still open. My dad made perfect sense, but trying to look and sound cheerful when you think you may have just lost a national election is not a particularly easy thing to do.

We were put to the test as soon as we landed in Austin. The conference room at campaign headquarters was overflowing with young staffers and volunteers, most of whom had been working nonstop for well over a year. They'd all heard about the exit polls and were more than a little worried. Dad thanked them for all their hard work, talked about what a rewarding experience being part of this campaign had been for our whole family, and told them that while it looked like it was going to be a close fight, he felt confident that George W. Bush was going to be the next president of the United States.

We also stopped by Karl Rove's office, and he said it was definitely going to be a late night. The race had tightened over the last few days, and Governor Bush definitely wasn't going to get the three-hundred-plus electoral votes we'd been so confidently predicting on the plane, but Karl was sure that the early exit polls were wrong and that we would win the election.

That afternoon was a lot like the afternoon before the VP debate—it seemed to last forever. Get-out-the-vote efforts were under way and the victory celebration down on Congress Avenue was all set up, so there really wasn't much left to do but wait for the polls to close. Mom and Dad did a few last-minute phone interviews with radio stations in some of the key battleground states, but the rest of us just sat in our hotel rooms, watching the clock, waiting for the first polls to close, and knowing that the outcome was completely out of our hands.

I turned on the TV to hear what the experts were saying. All the pundits were talking about Pennsylvania, Michigan, and Florida. The conventional wisdom was that if Vice President Gore won those three states, he would probably win the election. If we won any one of them, we'd probably win.

When the first polls finally closed, and the networks started calling states, I wasn't too surprised that Pennsylvania and Michigan went for Al Gore, but we were all surprised when they called Florida for him as well, particularly since the polls were still open in the state's Republican-friendly panhandle. Losing Florida wasn't necessarily a fatal blow, but it was close to one, and it certainly made it a lot tougher for us to win.

Our family was watching a bank of televisions that had been set up in my parents' hotel suite, but we also had well over a hundred friends and relatives gathered downstairs in a ballroom, eating dinner and watching election coverage on several large projection screen televisions. When the networks called Florida for Vice President Gore, my parents decided it was time to go downstairs to see everyone. My mother's brother, Mark Vincent, and his wife, Linda, were down there, as well as Dad's aunt, Ruth Dickey. Mom's aunts and uncles, Marion and Gerry Byron and Dale and Milly Vincent, had traveled from California and Virginia for election night. There were cousins from all over the country and friends from Wyoming like Dick and Maggie Scarlett, John and Mary Kay Turner, Jan and Jack Larimer, and Celeste and Dan Colgan, whom my parents had known for decades. There were people from my parents' early days in Washington, staffers from my dad's time in Congress and at the Pentagon, and friends they had made in Dallas. However the election turned out, my parents wanted to be sure all those people knew how much their support and friendship was appreciated. They asked Heather, Liz, Phil, and me if we would like to go downstairs with them, but none of us felt up to the challenge of being social. We decided to stay upstairs, watch the coverage, and hope for good news.

Our first indication that something might be going on in Florida was when we saw Mary Matalin on CNN. She said, with a good deal of feeling, that the networks' call, made while the polls in the panhandle were still open, was too early. She offered a small glimmer of hope that went against everything the exit polls and the experts were saying, and her words were roundly blasted by various network commentators as nothing more than desperate campaign spin. But then other campaign officials and Republican spokespeople began making the same point on other networks. It was hard to imagine that the networks would take back their call. Nobody could remember anything like that happening before, but we started to have some hope.

My parents came back upstairs from the ballroom party in a great mood. They'd heard the rumors that the networks might have been wrong about Florida, but more important, they'd spent time with friends. My mom insisted we go downstairs, promising it would cheer us up, so we humored her. When we got there, Florida was still in Al Gore's column, but everybody was pretty upbeat. All the talk about the networks' having made a mistake gave them something to pin their hopes on.

Then Voter News Service retracted their call on Florida, and all the networks followed suit. Florida was back in the toss-up column. Heather and I were talking to former senator Alan Simpson and his wife, Ann, when the news broke, and Senator Simpson grabbed us both up in a great big bear hug and said that he was sure this meant that we were going to win.

Someone made an announcement that the buses were leaving for the big celebration on Congress Avenue. We figured it wouldn't be too much longer before the final results were in, and while no one could guarantee we were going to win, having the networks take Florida back from Al Gore gave everyone a huge boost of confidence.

We went back upstairs to my parents' suite at nine-thirty. A few close friends were there as well: the Simpsons, former treasury secretary Nick Brady and his wife, Kitty; Jim and Susan Baker; Don and Joyce Rumsfeld; Don Evans, the chairman of the campaign; and Andy Card, who'd overseen the Republican National Convention. Everyone was pretty sure we'd be leaving shortly for the governor's mansion, but one hour passed, then two, then three. Florida was still a toss-up; neither Governor Bush nor Vice President Gore had locked up the electoral votes needed for victory.

A little before 1:00 A.M., Dad decided that he was going to take a nap. He told us to wake him if anything happened, and less than twenty minutes later, it did. At 1:16 A.M. Central Time, Fox News announced that Governor Bush had won the state of Florida, and within a few minutes, all the other networks followed suit. We had all been struggling to stay awake while we watched the returns roll in, but as soon as the networks announced that we'd won, Liz and I jumped up and down, and hugged everyone in the room. Mom woke up Dad, and Logan Walters, Governor Bush's personal aide, called to tell us that the governor wanted us all to come down to the mansion. It was one of the happiest moments of my life.

In all the commotion, I almost didn't notice Don Evans sitting at the table at the back of the room, talking on his cell phone. After he hung up, he told us that Bill Daley, Vice President Gore's campaign chairman, had called to let him know that Vice President Gore would be calling Governor Bush to concede very soon, but had asked that we please be patient and wait until after he made his concession speech before going out and declaring victory. The vice president was with his family, and they were understandably upset at losing the election. Daley said it might be a few minutes before he made the call. It sounded like a perfectly reasonable request.

By the time we arrived at the governor's mansion, Vice President Gore had called Governor Bush and officially conceded. George W. Bush was no longer being referred to as "Governor Bush." Everyone was calling him "Mr. President." The Bush family and a few key staffers like Karen Hughes were milling around downstairs, talking and laughing.

Our family joined the Bushes in the downstairs sitting room and huddled around a small TV set, waiting for Vice President

Gore to go onstage at the War Memorial in Nashville, Tennessee, and deliver his concession speech. We waited, then waited some more, but nothing happened. Something wasn't right. We had seen video of Al Gore arriving at the War Memorial and didn't understand why he hadn't appeared onstage. Then Vice President Gore called again, this time to tell George W. Bush that things had changed and that he was taking back his concession. Shortly afterward, the networks once again put Florida in the too-close-to-call column. It was stunning news.

Kathleen Shanahan and Governor Jeb Bush were using a laptop and a very slow dial-up connection to try to access information about what was going on from the Florida secretary of state's website or from the AP. Unfortunately, everyone else in the country who was still awake was doing the same thing and no one could get through. The last any of us had heard, we were leading in Florida by tens of thousands of votes, but now the networks were saying that at most, we were only ahead by a few thousand votes.

The Gore campaign sent Bill Daley out to address the Gore supporters gathered at the War Memorial. He announced that the race was too close to call and that "our campaign continues." There was some thought at the mansion that Governor Bush should declare victory, but that idea was quickly discarded in favor of having Don Evans go to Congress Avenue, where people had been waiting in the rain for hours, to address the crowd. Evans was just right for the job. He sounded calm and confident and not the least bit cocky or presumptuous when he said, "We hope and believe we have elected the next president of the United States." It was a good speech—but certainly not the victory celebration any of us had anticipated.

Our family finally went back to the hotel around 4:00 A.M. In a little less than twenty-four hours, I'd gone from being absolutely certain that we were going to win, to being fairly sure we were going

to lose, to watching as every major media outlet in the country declared my dad to be the vice president–elect of the United States, to
watching, less than two hours later, as the networks came back and
said, "Not necessarily." We were all stunned and exhausted, but at
most I figured it was going to be only another day or two before the
situation in Florida was resolved and we could finally celebrate a
Bush-Cheney victory.

At the start of the 1978 campaign on the front steps of our house in Casper, Wyoming: Cyrano—the family basset hound—with Mom, Dad, Liz, and me *(bottom left)*.
(David Hume Kennerly/Getty Images)

Fly-fishing on the Snake River in Wyoming a few days after the 2000 convention with Dad and Liz *(right)*.   (David Hume Kennerly/Getty Images)

At the 2000 convention in Philadelphia. My first day on the job as Dad's personal assistant. (DAVID HUME KENNERLY/GETTY IMAGES)

Briefing Dad, Gerry Parsky, the California state campaign chairman, and Colin Powell during a stop on a bus tour through southern California. They're straining to hear me over the marching band warming up on the other side of the bus. (M. SPENCER GREEN/THE ASSOCIATED PRESS)

Liz *(right)* and I celebrate as the networks declare George W. Bush and Dick Cheney to be the next president and vice president of the United States. Andy Card, Nick Brady, Alan Simpson, and James Baker III are standing behind us. (M. SPENCER GREEN/THE ASSOCIATED PRESS)

The big letdown as the recount begins—Dad and I watch the latest news reports with Scooter Libby and Steve Hadley in my parents' hotel room in Austin. (M. SPENCER GREEN/THE ASSOCIATED PRESS)

With campaign finance co-chairman Jack Oliver and Dad aboard *Air Force Two*.
(DAVID BOHRER/THE WHITE HOUSE)

On the way to a speech in Florida.
(DAVID BOHRER/THE WHITE HOUSE)

Aboard *Air Force Two*, staff secretary Neil Patel makes last-minute changes to Dad's speech while Scooter Libby, Anne Womack, and I offer suggestions. Dan Wilmot, director of vice presidential advance, can be seen in the background.
(DAVID BOHRER/THE WHITE HOUSE)

A few words with Dad before a town hall meeting with employees at a manufacturing plant in Missouri during the final few weeks of the 2004 campaign.
(DAVID BOHRER/THE WHITE HOUSE)

Mom and I laugh about a headline in the *Weekly World News* that declares: DICK CHENEY IS A ROBOT!
(DAVID BOHRER/THE WHITE HOUSE)

Briefing Mom and Dad on *Air Force Two*.
(David Hume Kennerly/Getty Images)

After the final presidential debate, I received a lot of attention, not all of it welcome. This sign at a rally in Grand Rapids, Michigan, helped lift my spirits.
(David Bohrer/The White House)

Election Day 2004: early in the morning at my parents' house in Jackson, Wyoming, Dad and I wait for the polls to open so he and Mom can go vote.
(David Bohrer/The White House)

Election night 2004: A little more than eighteen hours later, Liz and I are in the White House Residence, checking in with friends and various campaign staffers on our cell phones while we wait for the final results to come in. (David Bohrer/The White House)

Heather and I on our way to a black-tie dinner on the night before the inauguration.
(DAVID BOHRER/THE WHITE HOUSE)

January 20, 2005—I hold the family Bible and my mom and Liz look on while the Speaker of the House, Dennis Hastert, administers the oath of office. Mrs. Hastert, Senator Trent Lott, Jenna Welch (Laura Bush's mother), and the president can be seen behind us. (SUSAN STERNER/THE WHITE HOUSE)

CHAPTER 9

Thirty-seven More Days

Mom pulled open the drapes and announced, "That's it—we have to go outside." It had been three days since the election, and while George W. Bush was still leading in the vote count, there was no sign that the deadlock was going to be broken any time soon. Everyone in the family, except my dad, who'd been holding strategy meetings, had spent the last three days glued to the bank of televisions set up in my parents' hotel suite in Austin. We'd turn the volume up on Fox and watch that for a while, then mute everything but CNN, hoping against hope that somebody would have something new to report, but basically we were watching the same stories over and over again. So we wouldn't have to miss a minute of the news coverage, someone on the staff had arranged to have a room service cart magically appear outside the door every few hours filled with club sandwiches and Diet Cokes. Mom was right. We had to get out of the hotel—if only to find something other than club sandwiches to eat.

Unfortunately, there weren't a lot of options. My parents tried going for a walk and were quickly spotted by the press. Liz and Phil and Heather and I finally decided that a movie would probably be the safest bet—no one would notice us in a dark theater—so we borrowed a rental car and headed out to see *The Legend of Bagger Vance.* Admittedly, all we'd really done was trade one dark room with a big bright screen for another, but at least now we had popcorn and no one on the screen was talking about chads, butterfly ballots, or allegations of voter intimidation.

Part of what made those first few days so difficult was that everyone felt completely helpless—there was nothing that any of us could do but watch and wait for the results. I volunteered to go to Florida to help with the recount, but after a family discussion I was convinced—well, mostly convinced—that I really couldn't go. Since my father was one of the parties involved in the recount, I had a vested interest in the outcome and couldn't serve as a monitor while ballots were being counted. I understood the reasoning and didn't push the issue, but I kept thinking to myself that this was a presidential election, and everyone had a vested interest in the outcome. Besides, there had to be jobs other than ballot monitoring that needed to be done. Going to Florida to do anything had to be better than sitting in Austin doing nothing.

Dad was really the only member of our family who had something to do in those early days of the recount. Since the first morning after the election, he'd been holding meetings with Governor Bush, talking to his advisors, and conferring with former secretary of state James Baker, who had gone to Florida to oversee the recount effort.

Governor Bush had called Secretary Baker the morning after the election. The secretary was on his way back to Houston from Austin, but the governor prevailed on him to go to Florida, and it's hard to imagine anyone better to head up our efforts there. Jim Baker is one of the best political operatives ever, and tough enough to go toe-to-toe with the Democrats in a fight—which was exactly what Florida was shaping up to be.

As soon as it became obvious that the automatic recount was not going to overturn George W. Bush's victory, Bill Daley, chairman of the Gore campaign, held a press conference in Tallahassee and announced, "We are going to support legal actions," thus ending any hope for a quick, nonlawyerly resolution. The Democrats were going to conduct a no-holds-barred legal fight until they got the outcome they wanted.

Every day of the recount, Dad took part in conference calls with Governor Bush, Secretary Baker, and the legal team in Florida to discuss various issues and to plot out our own legal strategy. One of the first questions to be addressed was whether to pursue action in federal as well as in state court. Everyone agreed that federal court was a long shot but that we needed to try, particularly because the Florida State Supreme Court was generally considered one of the most liberal and Democrat-friendly courts in the country. One of the possible federal issues under discussion on those early calls was whether the fact that different counties had different standards for determining what constituted a vote opened the way for a Fourteenth Amendment "equal protection" case. Ultimately, these early federal arguments laid the groundwork for the final appeal to the United States Supreme Court, but, at the time, most people had little notion that the election would end up there.

One person who did was Alan Simpson. He came up to my parents' suite before leaving Austin and, while saying his good-byes, mentioned that he didn't know what route through the court the election dispute would take, or what the exact issue would be, but that he was sure that this election would end up in the U.S. Supreme Court. At the time it sounded a little melodramatic and sensational—but he was right.

The other key issue in the early days of the recount was what to do about the transition. Even without a recount, the winner would have had less than three months to get his administration in place. That may sound like a long time, and many Democrats claimed it was, which might have been true if they'd won, but the Republican Party had been out of power for eight years, and there were hundreds of key positions—including cabinet secretaries and national security officials—that would have to be filled by January 20, Inauguration Day. Every day that the recount dragged on made it much more difficult to reach that goal.

Several possibilities were discussed, including sending Dad out the day after the election to announce that the Bush administration was starting its transition immediately because of the importance of giving the new administration the full transition time. But I don't recall anyone arguing too strongly for this approach. The media, and possibly the American people, would have seen it as rushing and overreaching, so a compromise was devised. No formal announcement would be made—at least in the early days of the recount—but the transition would still go forward. Governor Bush asked Dad to oversee it, and the two of them quietly started filling key positions. It wasn't long before word of the operation leaked, and within a few days, every major news outlet reported that George W. Bush had already decided that Colin Powell would be the secretary of state, Condoleeza Rice would be the national security advisor, and Andy Card would be the White House chief of staff.

Trying to run a presidential transition under these circumstances was not an easy assignment, and looking back on it, I realize that my dad really was the perfect choice for the job. He'd been through changes of government before, from President Ford to Jimmy Carter while he was White House chief of staff, and from President George H. W. Bush to Bill Clinton while he was secretary of defense. Moreover, he doesn't leak to the media, understands the inner workings of Washington and the federal government, and has no desire to be in the spotlight—just the person you'd want to run an effective, low-key operation.

Our whole family wanted to stay in Austin until the results of the election were finalized. But it slowly became apparent that the recount was going to drag on much longer than any of us anticipated, and we knew that there were only so many days we could spend cooped up in the hotel. Heather and I were the first to fold. We drove home to Colorado the weekend after the election, calling back to Austin from the road every half hour, just in case something had changed. Liz and Phil left shortly thereafter so my nieces could go back to school. My parents hung in the longest. They stayed in Austin until November 18, a day that was supposed to be a very big one for the recount.

On that day, after all the absentee ballots had been counted, Katherine Harris, the Florida secretary of state, was supposed to certify the election results. Once George W. Bush was certified as the winner of Florida's electoral votes, the recount would be over. Vice President Gore could still contest the results of the election, but his chances of victory would be diminished since it would require a court decision to overturn the certification. But on the eighteenth, the Florida State Supreme Court stepped in and barred Katherine Harris from certifying the results. The justices set a new date for certification, November 26, effectively giving the counties that were conducting recounts eight more days to tally their results.

Arriving in Washington, my dad moved ahead with setting up a transition headquarters and staff. Under normal circumstances, he would have turned to the General Services Administration (GSA) for help. That's the federal agency charged with overseeing administrative functions for the federal government—everything from office space to computers to Post-it notes. After a presidential election, the GSA presents the winning candidate with the key to a transition office, which in 2000 was roughly ninety thousand square feet of furnished space in one of the federal office buildings in downtown Washington. GSA also provides access to federal funds that can be used to pay transition employees and associated costs. But because of the continuing recount, officials at the GSA announced that they would not turn over the keys or the money to either campaign. That meant that dad had to build a transition operation from scratch—with no office space, funding, or federal assistance of any kind.

The first Bush-Cheney transition office was the round wooden table in the kitchen of my parents' townhouse in McLean, Virginia. The staff consisted primarily of Liz, who had volunteered to help out, Scooter Libby, a close friend from my dad's days as secretary of defense and one of his advisors during debate prep, and Kathleen Shanahan, Dad's chief of staff on the campaign. Brian McCormack, who had replaced me as Dad's personal aide after the election, was also part of the team. Janet Rogers, my mom's best friend from college, made an invaluable contribution when she began showing up regularly with home-cooked food. Her help was especially appreciated since she brought the food all the way from her home in Annapolis, Maryland.

My parents had only one phone line in their house. Because cordless phones are just about the least secure type of phones to use, they went up to the attic and dug out an old beige eighties-style Princess phone, a relic from Liz's and my high school days. The ringer didn't work and the # button had a tendency to stick, but it was still better than the cordless phone they had in the kitchen, so it became Dad's phone for the transition. Everyone else had to rely on cell phones, and since no one could get a signal inside the house, people bunched up on the front porch or in the backyard trying to make calls.

The group had been hard at work for only a few days when the transition hit a bump in the road. My dad had a heart attack—sort of. He woke Mom up early on the morning of November 22 because he was experiencing some mild chest pain. Even though he knew it would become a huge news story, Dad did the smart and responsible thing and had the Secret Service agents on duty drive him and my mom to George Washington University Hospital, in Washington, D.C., so he could get checked out. Liz met them there, and Mom called me at home in Colorado. She said she didn't think it was anything to worry about, probably just a false alarm.

Initially, it looked like she was right. The doctors told my parents that the preliminary test results showed no sign of a heart attack, that it was probably just some mild angina. My mom and Liz helped Juleanna Glover, Dad's press secretary, prepare a media release stating that Dad had had some chest pains and had gone to the hospital as a precautionary measure, but that he hadn't had a heart attack. A few hours later, Governor Bush made a public appearance and said, "He did not have a heart attack." We all thought that was true. An initial EKG had shown no change, and blood tests that doctors conducted to test his cardiac enzymes showed none of the elevated levels that would signal damage to heart muscle—a heart attack, in other words.

What we didn't know is that the doctors had also given Dad a newer, more sophisticated test that can detect the most minute damage to heart muscle. The results showed a small amount of damage, so slight, in fact, that if the episode had happened a few years earlier, before the newer test was available, my dad would not have been diagnosed as having had a heart attack at all.

As soon as it was understood that Dad had had a heart attack, Liz and Mom contacted the communications staff back in Austin and told them that the doctors treating Dad were going to hold a press conference and would explain the entire situation—including the new test results. During the press conference, however, the doctors used medical jargon and terms like "elevated cardiac enzyme levels," but they never actually said the words "heart attack." As soon as the press conference was over, Karen Hughes called Liz to tell her that reporters didn't understand that "elevated cardiac enzyme levels" meant "heart attack." Karen wanted the doctors to hold another press conference to clear up the confusion, and, she said, they had to use the words "heart attack."

Liz, who stood in the back of the room at the second press conference, observed later that it was like watching a National Geographic Special on sharks. The reporters were in a feeding frenzy, shouting at the doctors and demanding to know if the Bush-Cheney campaign was trying to cover up Dad's condition. It was awful, but at least we finally had all of the information out, and Dad felt pretty good—which was the most important thing.

All of this happened on the Wednesday before Thanksgiving, a day when my dad usually cooks up a full turkey dinner with all the trimmings. He's the cook in the family, and a pretty good one, too, but now he was out of action. I'm the other family member who likes to cook, but I was at home in Colorado with Heather and her family. Since my mom was at the hospital with Dad, that meant that if there was going to be a Thanksgiving dinner, Liz would have to cook it.

I love my sister very much. She is an incredibly talented, smart, and impressive individual, but she had never cooked a Thanksgiving dinner in her life. To help her, my dad sat up in his hospital bed, took a page of talking points that the campaign had put together about his heart attack, and wrote out detailed directions on how to cook a turkey on the back. To make sure that there weren't any mistakes, he wrote down every possible step, including "Take the plastic wrapping off the turkey." Liz and Kathleen Shanahan were on the way to the grocery store to pick up all the necessary ingredients when Liz's cell phone rang. It was Alma Powell, Colin Powell's wife, offering to cook a turkey for our family. It was an incredibly generous and gracious gesture.

Liz was telling Mrs. Powell how much she appreciated the offer, but that she didn't want to impose, when Kathleen tapped her on the arm and whispered, "Are you crazy? Accept." And she did. When Liz went over to the Powells' the next day to pick up the turkey, she was amazed to discover that in addition to the turkey, Mrs. Powell, who was also cooking for her own family, had prepared stuffing, potatoes, and gravy for our family—a second entire Thanksgiving dinner. Liz thanked her profusely, and to this day whenever I see Alma Powell I always think of her kindness to our family.

Thanksgiving dinner was served buffet-style in the hospital room next to Dad's. As it was described to me over the phone, between the food Alma Powell had prepared and the dishes contributed by some wonderful friends of Kathleen, there was more than enough to feed our family, staff members, friends, and the Secret Service agents who were working that day.

After he was released from the hospital on November 24, Dad immediately went back to work on the transition. November 26 was the new deadline for the certification of Florida's election results, and if everything went as expected, Governor Bush would be certified the winner of Florida's twenty-five electoral votes. We all assumed that Vice President Gore would contest the certification, but having it would put us a step closer to finally and officially being declared the winners—and it would also, we hoped, prompt the GSA to give us the office space that was set aside for the transition. The kitchen in McLean was getting pretty crowded.

On the night of November 26, the Florida State Elections Commission, presided over by Katherine Harris, certified George W. Bush as the winner of the state's presidential election. The margin of victory was 537 votes. In McLean, Liz woke up her oldest daughter, Kate, who was then six years old, to tell her that Grandpa had been elected vice president of the United States. Kate rolled over and said, "Again?"

That night Governor Bush gave a televised victory speech. He also officially named Dad as the head of the transition operation and asked him to work with the Clinton administration to open the transition offices in Washington, D.C. A few hours later a White House spokesperson announced that, regardless of the certification, the administration was unwilling to turn over either the office space or the federal funds set aside to help pay for the costs of the transition until all the legal challenges had been resolved.

At that point, Liz volunteered to find some office space near the house. Working with Bobbi Kilberg and Jerry Halprin, a couple of longtime Bush supporters, she quickly found a building that would work, and in just a few days the team installed a phone system, rented office furniture, and hired a firm to provide security.

Since GSA was still refusing to provide any financial support for the transition, the Bush-Cheney campaign created a foundation to help pay for expenses. Donations were capped at five thousand dollars, and no corporate or political action committee money was accepted. It wasn't the first time a campaign raised money to help pay for a transition—Bill Clinton raised over $5 million in 1992, but at least he got some assistance from GSA. We were completely on our own.

The official start of the transition marked the culmination of what the staff referred to as "The Flag Wars." It had started simply enough. Early in the recount effort, the advance team put out one flag to serve as a backdrop when Secretary Baker made a public statement; then we noticed that the Gore campaign had two flags at their next press conference, so we upped our number to five. When Vice President Gore went on national television to explain why he was contesting the certification, he had seven American flags behind him. Later that day, at Dad's press conference there were fourteen. One of our advance men had found a "flag cannon" that could hold seven flags, so he had put a splendid array of two cannon behind Dad. At that point, the media started reporting on how many flags were at each press conference rather than what was said, so Dad announced that there would be no more than two flags at future press conferences.

Having spent the past four weeks watching television in Colorado, I wanted to do something—anything—to help, so I flew to D.C. and volunteered at the transition offices. The first thing I noticed was how many people were helping out, not just staff from the campaign and donors and supporters from the Washington area, but longtime friends of my parents like Mary Kay Turner, who had come all the way from Jackson, Wyoming. The headquarters were pretty Spartan—thinly furnished, and not many pictures on the wall, though my dad did have one I loved a lot. It was taken by Mike Green, a photographer from AP who frequently traveled with us during the campaign, and showed an old wreck of a car with a great big sign on top that said "God Bless Dick Cheney" that someone had driven round and round George Washington Hospital during the couple of days that Dad had been a patient.

My dad was holding meeting after meeting in his office about the transition, but out in the hallways, most of the conversations were about Florida. One of the most interesting I had was with Barbara Olson, the author who was killed nine months later when Flight 77 crashed into the Pentagon. She introduced herself and asked if I wanted a souvenir ballot from Florida. She didn't look at the ballot as she handed it to me, and as far as I could tell, didn't do anything out of the ordinary—but she had somehow managed to partially punch out the number-five chad on the ballot. If it had been a real ballot, she would have just created a vote for Al Gore. That single gesture was the best argument anyone could make for the need to stop the endless recounts. Continued handling of the ballots wasn't finding more votes—it was creating them.

In early December, the United States Supreme Court weighed in for the first time, and voted 9–0 to set aside the Florida Supreme Court's ruling extending the deadline for recount results and to send the issue back to the Florida court for further clarification. In Leon County, Judge Sanders Sauls refused to overturn the certification of George W. Bush as the winner in Florida, and the Gore campaign immediately appealed the decision to the Florida Supreme Court.

The Florida justices heard arguments on Thursday, December 7, and were scheduled to hand down their decision by 4:00 P.M. Friday. Everyone at the transition offices expected the court to rule in our favor. Although the Florida court had a reputation as one of the most liberal in the country, we thought it would have a hard time overturning Judge Sauls's decision. We were ready for the postelection drama to finally be over. We'd been close several times before and had even gotten to the point of collecting money and printing up flyers for the victory celebration—but this time, we were sure. We were finally going to win.

On Friday afternoon, I picked up Heather at the airport and we raced back to the transition office to watch the announcement of the court decision. We were all stunned when the Florida Supreme Court not only ruled in Al Gore's favor, but went beyond what the

Gore legal team had asked for and ordered an immediate statewide recount of more than forty-five thousand undervotes—ballots that registered no vote for president. The Bush legal team immediately appealed the decision to the U.S. Court of Appeals for the Eleventh Circuit and filed a request for a stay with the U.S. Supreme Court.

The vote counting in Florida started first thing Saturday morning and was supposed to last until Sunday afternoon. Knowing that there really wasn't anything that any of us could do to affect matters, our family—including my parents—all went to see a Saturday matinee of *Proof of Life,* starring Meg Ryan and Russell Crowe, not a great movie, but a good distraction, and as the credits rolled, all of our cell phones started ringing. The U.S. Supreme Court had issued a stay, halting the recount in Florida. Back at the transition office, everyone was happy about the decision, but cautious. We'd been burned so many times before—getting our hopes up, thinking it might be over—only to have the Gore campaign come back to life. We'd gotten the stay, but we still had to win the argument in front of the Supreme Court.

Early Monday morning, Heather and I drove down to the Court with Liz and Phil. We entered through a back entrance, because thousands of protesters had gathered out front. It looked like a huge political circus—people were carrying placards that said things like "Sore-Loserman," "Military Moms for Bush," and "Count Every Vote." Gore supporters were yelling at Bush supporters, who were yelling right back. Representatives from the National Black Farmers Association even brought a live mule to the protest—I never did figure out why.

The scene inside the courtroom was equally entertaining. Most people were in their seats by the time we got there, but Jesse Jackson was working the crowd, and from where we were sitting, it looked like he managed to say hello to just about every Democratic official in the room. There was no separate seating for Republicans and Democrats, so there were all sorts of strange pairings—Liz sat next to the wife of Alan Dershowitz, one of the lead attorneys for Al Gore, and Bobbi Kilberg, one of the people who helped find the space for the transition office in McLean, sat with three of the four Gore children.

I'd never watched oral arguments in front of the Supreme Court before and was amazed at the way the justices fired questions at the attorneys. My favorite moment, and one of the most telling, came during a discussion of what standard should be used to determine what constituted a vote. Justice O'Connor asked David Boies, the attorney for Vice President Gore, "Well, why isn't the standard the one that voters are instructed to follow, for goodness' sakes? I mean, it couldn't be clearer." The justices pushed hard at all three lawyers—David Boies; Ted Olson, representing George W. Bush; and Joseph Klock, representing the Florida secretary of state. When the session was over, Mindy Tucker, one of the campaign's communications staffers, stopped us on our way out and asked us how it went. Liz and I said that we thought we'd won, but that we wouldn't know for sure until we heard the decision.

The justices handed down their decision the following evening, December 12. Seven of the nine justices ruled that the recount was unconstitutional because inconsistent and changing standards were being used to count the ballots. In addition, the Justices ruled 5–4 that a recount meeting constitutional standards would not be possible before the December 12 deadline for states to choose their electors and that therefore the recount must stop. It took a while for all of the experts and analysts to work their way through the sixty-five-page decision and explain what it meant, but when they did, it was clear that it was finally over—we'd won.

The mood at my parents' house was surprisingly subdued. Dad

stayed up to watch the coverage, but Mom was fast asleep in bed. Heather had already flown home to Colorado, and I was sick with the flu and completely miserable. The first people to congratulate my dad weren't even Cheneys—they were photographers. David Kennerly, a photographer for *Newsweek* who had been President Ford's White House photographer, and Mike Green, from AP, were at a nearby restaurant when the decision came out, and they raced over to our house to take some pictures and congratulate my dad. Not long after, Liz and Phil showed up with a bottle of champagne and everyone drank a toast to President George W. Bush and Vice President Dick Cheney.

We held a real celebration the following night. Even though it was the hectic Christmas party season, the campaign managed to find a free hotel ballroom, and everyone—staff, volunteers, donors—who had helped make the victory possible was invited. My family watched Al Gore's concession speech and George Bush's acceptance speech with a few friends—including Paul Wolfowitz; Scooter Libby and his wife, Harriet Grant; Barbara and Ted Olson; Joanne and Jack Kemp; and Colin and Alma Powell—in a suite upstairs. Dad agreed to let a small pool of photographers and cameramen into the room during part of Vice President Gore's speech. Fortunately, they left just before my three-year-old niece, Elizabeth, walked in.

She was holding a piece of bread in one hand and a sippy cup full of milk in the other as she strolled over to the television, stared up at it for a few seconds, and then announced in an incredibly loud voice, "I don't like Al Gore." We all laughed, but it wasn't a moment you wanted preserved on videotape, at least not when Al Gore had just conceded and, in fact, given one of the most graceful speeches of his career.

There were lots of hugs and even a few tears at the celebration party, as well as a strong sense of relief that the recount and the court cases were finally over. But one of the best moments of the whole ordeal came the next day when Thurman Davis, deputy administrator of the GSA, finally presented my dad with the keys to the official transition office space at Eighteenth and G Streets, just a few blocks from the White House. It was just a small plastic key card on a lanyard, but after weeks of waiting, it looked mighty good.

Inauguration morning, the women in my family emerged from my parents' townhouse dressed and groomed to the nines. My mom was wearing a great-looking green coat with a fur collar that Kwon Suk Im, a designer and friend, had made for her. We'd all had our hair done by Paul Ramadan, a terrific hairdresser who'd come to my mother's rescue in the middle of the campaign when details of her visits to the Georgetown salon she had been using started to appear in the *Washington Post.* We'd even been ministered to by a professional makeup artist. My dad, in a dark suit and coat, looked pretty much as usual, though maybe his smile was just a little bit bigger.

Our first stop was St. John's, the historic yellow stucco church across from the White House on Lafayette Square, for a service of prayer and song. Afterward, my parents were supposed to go straight to the White House, but the Clintons, to no one's great surprise, were running late, so my parents and the Bushes waited in the cars outside St. John's for about twenty minutes until they were ready. Liz, Heather, Phil, and I went on up to the Capitol and sat in a big windowless room known as EF 100 that has been used as a holding area since Ronald Reagan's first inaugural. Once my parents and the Bushes arrived, we were escorted through the Capitol building and announced onto the ceremonial platform for the swearing-in.

It rained off and on during the inaugural ceremony, and if you look at the pictures, you can see that everyone's hairdos and makeup wilted pretty fast. But you can also see that none of us cared about the weather. We thought it was a pretty nice day as we stood on the inaugural platform with my dad and watched him take the oath of office as vice president of the United States.

CHAPTER 10

Re-election

I had thought that the 2000 campaign was my swan song in presidential politics. When it was over, I went back to business school, and when I graduated in the summer of 2002, I was contemplating a couple of job prospects that seemed pretty good—though, I have to confess, none as exciting as working on a national campaign. In September 2002, my dad and I were sitting on the front porch of the Vice President's Residence—a beautiful old Victorian house that sits on a hill on the grounds of the United States Naval Observatory—discussing what I was going to do with my life now that I had my MBA, when he asked me if I'd want to work on another political campaign. I told him it all depended. I explained that working on the 2000 campaign had been a highlight of my life—the fast pace of it, the pressure of working under tight deadlines, and the opportunity to work with an incredibly talented and impressive group of people. But most of all, I told him, I'd loved working for him.

There are professional political consultants who spend their careers working on different campaigns for different candidates, but I don't think I'm cut out for that. I love campaigns, but it would take a very special candidate to get me to give up a year or two of my life to work for them. It would take a candidate that I believe in as strongly as I believe in my father.

We talked about campaigns and candidates for a while and then Dad said, "How about coming to work for me on the re-election?" He explained that he needed someone to run Vice Presidential Operations at the campaign and that he thought I'd be the best fit. I'd been through the 2000 campaign and already knew and had worked with a lot of the people who would be involved with the re-election. I knew what had worked well for my parents in 2000, and had an idea about what could be improved upon in 2004. And, most important, I understood the world of the vice presidency.

I've never seen anyone associated with the White House or either of the campaigns slight my dad, and certainly President Bush never has, but in a presidential campaign, nearly everyone's focus is on the guy at the top of the ticket—as it should be. The vice presidential candidate tends to be a bit of an afterthought. My parents needed at least one person at the campaign who was focused on them. I loved the idea of being that person, and told my dad that I thought it sounded great, but that I needed to talk to Heather before I could commit to another national campaign.

I had been on the road for three and a half months during the 2000 campaign, and the only reason I'd been able to be away from home for that long was because I had a generous partner who took care of everything from paying the bills to dealing with frozen pipes while I was gone. If I went to work on the re-election campaign, I'd be away from home for at least a year and a half. Heather wasn't thrilled at the idea of my being gone for so long, but she also knew how much my dad asking me to oversee his campaign operation meant to me. "If you don't do it," she said, "you'll always regret it. I think you should go ahead." With her blessing, I told Dad that I'd take the job.

The campaign wouldn't start officially until the spring of 2003, but during the intervening months, Dad and I had several conversations about how the campaign would be organized. What he wanted was what he had worked to put in place in the White House: a system for running his office that not only supported him, but that was also totally supportive of the president's efforts.

Traditionally, during a national campaign, vice presidential candidates are heard from twice—when they give their acceptance speech at the national convention and at the vice presidential debate. They spend the rest of the time traveling around safe states firing up the base and trying not to make too much news. It's also not unusual for the vice presidential candidate and his staff to find themselves excluded from the inner circle of the campaign where the strategy is formed and the decisions are made. This is largely because vice presidential nominees tend to be people who have their own presidential aspirations, and, even if the two candidates get along with each other, there usually isn't a whole lot of trust between presidential and vice presidential campaign staffs. If it's the ticket's first run for national office, the VP nominee may have been the presidential candidate's opponent during the primaries. If it's a re-election, the vice president may be more interested in lining up support for his own presidential run four years hence than in helping the president win re-election.

It's a relationship that can be strained even after the election is won. After being sworn into office, vice presidents have usually been relegated to the sidelines, where they just don't get to do very much. When asked to name a major decision that Richard Nixon, his vice president, had participated in, President Eisenhower responded, "If you give me a week, I might think of one." Vice President Truman didn't learn about the Manhattan Project, the military's highly classified program to build the first atomic bomb, until after President Roosevelt died and he was sworn in to replace him. Until Walter Mondale was sworn into office in 1977, no vice president even had an office in the West Wing of the White House.

From the beginning, George W. Bush had made it clear that he wasn't looking for a traditional vice president and that he had chosen my dad as his running mate not for political reasons, but because Dad was fully qualified to serve as president and would be a valuable asset once they were in the White House. After Dad was nominated, everyone on the Bush campaign, from the governor on down, went out of their way to make sure that our family felt welcome and that we, along with everyone on Dad's staff, were included as part of the team. Once they were sworn in, Dad made sure that his staff worked closely with President Bush's staff to help support and promote the president's agenda. It was a very effective system, and it was an approach that Dad wanted to continue during the re-election campaign. As director of VP Operations, I would be in charge of Dad's side of the campaign, everything from scheduling and budget, to hiring a staff and overseeing his campaign events. My focus would be on my parents and whatever they needed, but I was also responsible for making sure that VP Operations did everything possible to support the overall campaign.

By the time Dad was named as the vice presidential nominee in July 2000, the Bush campaign was well established, and the campaign headquarters in Austin was already up and running; staffers were in place and they'd been working together since well before the first primary. This time around, it would be different. This time around we'd get to be a part of the campaign from the beginning.

My first day in the headquarters was June 10, 2003, four weeks after Bush-Cheney '04 Inc. filed papers with the Federal Election Commission and seventeen months before Election Day. A small contingent of campaign staff had just moved into offices in Arlington, Virginia, across the Potomac from the White House. The night before the office opened, Ken Mehlman, the campaign manager, and Kelley McCullough, the deputy campaign manager for Operations, worked late into the night putting yellow sticky notes on all of the doors and cubicles so that everyone knew where they were supposed to go. Unfortunately, the Post-its had a tendency to fall off whenever anyone walked by or when the air-conditioner was blowing just a bit too hard. This meant that if you wanted to find someone, you had to look at all the Post-its lying around on the floor until you found the right one, and then you had to look in all the surrounding offices and cubicles until you found the person you needed. After about a week of this, someone on the staff decided to fix the system and made computer-generated name tags that they laminated to the walls and doors using several rolls of scotch tape. The new name tags didn't fall off, but they were pretty tough to move if you ever had to change offices.

As with any start-up operation, the first weeks of the campaign were spent setting up offices and filling jobs. There were twenty to thirty full-time employees when I first started, mostly senior staff and finance people. By Election Day, that number would expand to over three hundred. VP Operations would eventually grow to include several full advance teams and a handful of event coordinators to handle all of the rallies, town hall meetings, and speeches on Dad's schedule. The first position I had to fill was a staff assistant for VP Ops, someone who could help me with budget tracking and travel arrangements for the advance teams. There were several candidates, but most of the recent college graduates I interviewed didn't want to be a staff assistant—at least not for any length of time. They saw the job as a stepping-stone to a more prestigious position in the campaign, something like campaign manager or director of strategy. After one young woman told me that she was really interested only in positions that could offer her "opportunities for personal growth and job security," I explained to her that this was a political campaign, and that while the person hired for this position might grow personally and professionally, that wasn't the goal. The goal was to re-elect the president. And as for job security, come November 3, whether we won or lost, she would be unemployed. She didn't get the job. Instead I hired Taylor Talt, a smart, friendly, organized young man who had just graduated from the University of Southern California, where he had played football. Taylor was a hard worker, willing to do whatever needed to be done, from autopenning photos of my dad and arranging last-minute travel for advance people, to helping plan routes for bus tours. He was a great addition to VP Operations.

I also hired two deputy directors for VP Operations. The first, Elizabeth Mason, had been on one of the advance teams in 2000 and had worked as the director of scheduling and advance for my mom during the first term. She came on board to oversee my mom's campaign events and to help out with arrangements for friends, family, and other VIPs at major events such as the convention, the debate, and election night. Her familiarity with my mom's office and with our family was invaluable.

Kara Ahern, a Boston native, was the second deputy I hired. I had worked with her on several fundraising events when she was regional finance director for the re-election and I convinced her to come over to VP Operations. She was smart, funny, calm in a crisis, and had a great eye for events. She managed most of the logistics for Dad's campaign stops and always found creative ways to keep events looking new and fresh—such as holding a town hall meeting in a Cabelas sporting goods store with stuffed elk and caribou as the backdrop, or using the picturesque town square in Ligonier, Pennsylvania, as a stop on one of our bus tours.

Not every assignment on a political campaign is exciting and interesting, but they are all important, and the most valuable employees are willing to do whatever it takes to get the job done. This point was brought home to me during my first week on the job when I walked into Ken Mehlman's office to ask him a question. One of the office interns was sitting quietly next to Ken's desk, holding a pair of scissors, and whenever Ken handed him a piece of paper, the intern would cut it into dozens and dozens of small pieces. I asked what was going on, and Ken explained that the paper shredders hadn't shown up yet, so he was making do with a human paper shredder. As I watched the intern cut up another piece of paper, I couldn't help but admire his work ethic and think that here was a person who deserved a chance for some personal and professional growth.

The campaign had to overcome one other equipment problem in the first few weeks. The phones that the campaign installed were fairly standard office models that had the numbers printed on oversized gray rubber buttons. If a staffer was trying to make a long-distance call, he or she would have to dial a 9 to get an outside line, followed by a 1, the area code, and the number—nothing too complicated or challenging. But the buttons on the phones had a tendency to stick, so people kept accidentally dialing 9,911, the emergency number for the Arlington Police Department. Realizing that they'd misdialed, the staffers would automatically hang up and start over. Unfortunately, that didn't stop the calls from going through, and the Arlington police eventually complained about the number of 911 calls they were receiving from the campaign. To correct the situation, the number for getting an outside line was changed to 8. It was easier than replacing all the phones.

There would be lots of changes over the course of the campaign—new people would be hired and trained, new systems would be installed and refined, and the focus of our efforts would evolve from fundraising to the Democratic primaries to the general election. But one thing was constant throughout the entire eighteen months: the weekly all-staff meeting. Every Wednesday morning at nine, Ken Mehlman would gather every staff member and intern in one of the conference rooms at campaign headquarters. After he gave some brief remarks, he'd go around the room asking new people to introduce themselves and division directors to give an update on what was going on in their department. Sometimes guest speakers like Karl Rove or Andy Card would stop by to thank everyone for all of their hard work.

The meetings rarely lasted more than fifteen or twenty minutes, but they gave every staffer the opportunity to learn what was going on elsewhere in the campaign and helped everyone from the most senior people to the interns manning the phone banks feel like they were part of the team. The meetings were also crucial in helping to overcome a challenge faced by every re-election campaign: the potential conflict of two competing centers of power, the White House and the campaign. The White House, focused on governing, has to address issues that might not be the most advantageous to the campaign. The campaign, focused on turning out the vote and motivating the base, wants the candidate to devote time to matters that will help win on Election Day. It's the difference between the president addressing the United Nations General Assembly, which he has to do every September, and speaking at a meeting of the National Rifle Association.

A natural rivalry tends to develop between the campaign and White House staffs. Frequently, the staffers in the White House helped run and win the first campaign, and they have been known to say things like "Four years ago, we did it this way." And since people from the campaign don't have a White House ID hanging around their necks, they sometimes feel underappreciated or like second-class citizens. More than one frustrated campaign staffer has uttered the words "Don't they get it? If we don't win, they don't have a job."

Whenever Karl Rove and Andy Card stopped by the weekly meetings, their words of encouragement and inspiration helped knit the two sides together and make us all feel we were part of the same team. And Karl and Ken did something else that was absolutely critical to the success of the campaign. They encouraged a relentless focus on the goal—victory in November. Day in and day out, they concentrated on winning the election, and that helped everyone else—from senior staffers to brand-new interns—do exactly the same thing.

Running for re-election is complicated in ways that running from the outside is not. Of the forty-two men who have served as president, only sixteen have been elected to more than one term in office. Between 1980 and 2000, four presidents ran for re-election. Two won (Ronald Reagan and Bill Clinton), and two lost (Jimmy Carter and George H. W. Bush).

Incumbents do have a great advantage in congressional and senatorial races. They win well over 90 percent of the time. And while being an incumbent president is clearly a plus when it comes to name recognition and fundraising, holding the highest office also presents its challenges.

For one thing, you bear responsibility for everything that has happened during your first term in office—or in the case of George Bush and Dick Cheney, for things that happened even before that, namely, the close election in 2000. There were a number of people, some of them very well financed, who were still furious about the outcome of the 2000 election, and who were willing to spend a great deal of their own time and money to help defeat George W. Bush. There was also the fact that a recession had kicked in shortly after President Bush assumed office. The effects of it were made worse by the aftermath of 9/11, and unemployment had gone up, particularly in the manufacturing sector. Throughout the campaign the Democrats charged that the Bush administration was the first since Herbert Hoover's to have a net loss of jobs—a charge that ultimately proved to be untrue, but that during the campaign was an effective bit of rhetoric.

But the war was the big issue in 2004. Between the time the United States invaded Iraq in March 2003 and the presidential election, there was a significant fall-off in public support for the war because of concern about the continuing insurgency, the failure to find stockpiles of weapons of mass destruction, and the loss of American lives. The Democrats did everything they could to make the case that the Bush administration had mishandled the war and that a Kerry administration would have done better. How many times did I hear John Kerry proclaim on the nightly news that if he'd been president, the United States would have captured Osama bin Laden at Tora Bora?

These attacks would have been much more effective if Senator Kerry had been able to explain exactly what his position on the liberation of Iraq was, or if he'd laid out a clear plan showing what he would have done differently. Fortunately for us, he couldn't and didn't. During a photo op at the Grand Canyon, he was asked by a reporter if, knowing what he knew now, he would still have voted to support the invasion of Iraq. When he answered "yes," he undercut his attacks on President Bush completely. When it came to rousing Republican audiences, that response was second only to his famous proclamation about voting for the $87 billion to support our troops in Iraq before he voted against it. The crowds at our rallies never tired of hearing my dad mock that Kerry line.

The communications and rapid response teams at the campaign and at the Republican National Committee (RNC) did an outstanding job of highlighting Senator Kerry's inconsistencies and underscoring the president's record of leadership. Their efforts helped negate the constant barrage of Democratic attacks on the Bush administration's record and made the war into an issue that cut for us instead of against us—as it might have done if the Democrats had had a stronger candidate.

Incumbents also have a responsibility to continue governing during the campaign, and, as I realized when it came to scheduling events for my dad, that can pose challenges. According to the Constitution, the vice president also serves as the president of the Senate, a job that has one main responsibility: to cast the deciding vote in case of a tie. With the Senate closely divided, my dad had to be available whenever there was a possibility that he might have to cast a tie-breaking vote. For most of 2003 and 2004, we had to schedule his campaign trips either when the Senate was in recess or when there were no votes scheduled to take place.

By contrast, Senators Kerry and Edwards were rarely in Washington, D.C., or on Capitol Hill during 2003 and 2004. If there was a high-profile bill before the Senate, particularly one with big political implications, such as the $87-billion supplemental appropriation for the War on Terror, they would show up to cast their votes and offer their opinions, but for the most part, they spent their time campaigning, not serving in the Senate.

Still, incumbency does have its advantages, and perhaps nothing typifies them more than *Air Force One* and *Air Force Two,* the blue-and-white planes with tall black letters running down the length of the fuselage spelling out "United States of America." When Liz and I first boarded one of the C-32s that usually serve as *Air Force Two,* we both had the same reaction: So *this* is how the Gores got to campaign. A military version of the Boeing 757, it was a world removed from the rattling old chartered 727 that we had used in the 2000 campaign. It was comfortable, designed for long flights, and all of the equipment worked. There were no leaking fluids and no strange, unexplained noises when it landed. Instead of a genial but usually harried flight crew waving good-bye to my dad as he got off the plane, two uniformed airmen stood at attention at the bottom of the steps and saluted smartly as he passed by.

The 747s that usually serve as *Air Force One* are even more impressive. I've never met anyone who has watched *Air Force One* come in for a landing and not been awestruck. And, that, of course, is great for a campaign. For national security reasons, the president and the vice president always travel on military planes, even when they are running for re-election, and *Air Force One* and *Air Force Two* thrill waiting crowds. They cheer for the planes, and pictures of the landings are featured on the evening news and in the morning papers. The planes symbolize authority and stature, as do the motorcades and the presidential and vice presidential seals that go on every podium. These trappings of office are clearly a campaign asset.

But perhaps the most important advantage to being an incumbent is that you are there when history happens. On your watch, the country will face challenges, foreign and domestic, and the American people will see you responding as a leader. It's possible to fail the test, of course, but after 9/11, one of the great consequential events of our time, President Bush inspired the nation, particularly as he stood on the rubble at Ground Zero and told the rescue workers, "I can hear you. The rest of the world hears you, and the people who knocked these buildings down will hear all of us soon." That was on a Friday, and the following Sunday, people drew great comfort from my dad's appearance on Tim Russert's *Meet the Press*. He was knowledgeable about terrorists and their organizations, realistic that defeating terrorism would take years, and determined that we would defeat our terrorist foes and call to account those who supported them.

There are also times that are beyond politics when elected leaders can rise above differences. One of those was when former president Ronald Reagan's body was brought to lie in state in the rotunda of the United States Capitol. My dad delivered the eulogy, and although it was only a few minutes in length, it was very powerful. The speech did a wonderful job of capturing Ronald Reagan's spirit and his impact on this country and on the world. There were many touching lines and passages, but my favorite came near the end when Dad said, "It was the vision and will of Ronald Reagan that gave hope to the oppressed, shamed the oppressors, and ended an evil empire. More than any other influence, the Cold War was ended by the perseverance and courage of one man who answered falsehood with truth, and overcame evil with good." It was a fitting salute to a great man and a great president, and it was one of the finest speeches my dad has ever given.

Incumbents do get the blame when things go wrong, particularly with the economy, but they also get credit when things go right, as they did pretty remarkably at the end of 2003. In December my dad was supposed to attend a fundraiser in New York, just outside the city. I'd gone up early to help with all of the arrangements and was waiting for him when I got a call on my cell phone from Jen Field, Dad's personal aide. She was calling to let me know that they had just landed at the local airport, but that Dad was on an important call and would probably be a little late. I told her that everyone seemed to be enjoying themselves, so an extra fifteen or twenty minutes wouldn't be a problem. Then fifteen minutes turned into an hour and a half, and he was still sitting on the plane talking on the phone. I knew that it had to be something important and that there wasn't anything I could do to speed up the process, so I asked our host to stand up, say a few words, and let everyone know that the vice president had been unexpectedly delayed, but was on his way. All the guests were incredibly nice and patient and gave Dad a very warm welcome when he finally arrived.

Dad hates being late, so I expected him to be in a bit of a bad mood and to try and rush through the fundraiser, but he didn't. He was in a great mood. He took his time in the photo op and gave a wonderful off-the-cuff speech that the crowd loved.

Once we were on *Air Force Two* heading back to D.C., Dad suggested that we drop by the Rumsfelds' Christmas party when we got in. My mom was already there, he noted, so why didn't we join her? Given that it was already after nine o'clock and he'd just been at a fundraiser shaking hands and making small talk, it seemed like a strange suggestion. I figured the last thing he'd want to do was go to another party with even more people who'd want to make small talk, but I told him it sounded like fun, and I alerted the rest of the staff and the Secret Service to the change of plans.

We took the helicopter from Andrews Air Force Base to the Naval Observatory, and as we were walking from the helicopter to the limo, Dad told me there was news out of Iraq, but that I needed to keep it to myself since it hadn't yet been confirmed. I said I would. With all the people around him, we couldn't have a conversation, so when we got in the car, he handed me a note saying that American forces had captured a "high-value target" south of Tikrit, made preliminary identification, and were waiting for final DNA confirmation. Our troops had Saddam Hussein in custody, in other words, and would be announcing his capture as soon as the DNA results came through. It was great news, and now I understood why Dad had been late to the fundraiser and why he felt like celebrating. I had a thousand questions that I wanted to ask, but I couldn't, so we went to the Christmas party, and I didn't say a word.

Understandably Dad and Don Rumsfeld were in great moods at the party, and the evening ended with me, Dad, Mom, and the Rumsfelds sitting around a coffee table telling stories about the days when Dad worked for Rumsfeld at the Office of Economic Opportunity and in the Ford White House. It wasn't until we got back to the Vice President's Residence that Dad finally had the chance to tell Mom the news about Saddam Hussein. She was glad, of course, and impressed at how close to the chest my dad plays his cards.

Several hours later when the world learned that Saddam was in custody, there was a real feeling of euphoria across the nation. People were proud of the men and women of America's armed forces, and, as we headed into 2004, they were also proud of their commander-in-chief, George W. Bush.

CHAPTER 11

The Rules

Every aspect of the Bush-Cheney re-election campaign had its rules, but the most detailed guidelines were the ones regarding what could and could not happen at campaign events, including:

- No more than ten people may greet the principal upon arrival at an event. All exceptions must be approved in advance by either the campaign or the White House.
- The Pledge of Allegiance, prayers, and musical entertainment should take place before the principal goes onstage.
- Introductions should be under a minute in length and need to be submitted for approval before the event—shorter is always better.

All of these rules were designed to ensure that events ran smoothly, that everyone stayed on schedule, and that unanticipated incidents were kept to an absolute minimum. Some rules, such as the requirement that everyone who was onstage at a campaign event be vetted and cleared in advance, came from the White House, usually from either the Office of Presidential Advance or the Office of Political Affairs. Others, such as the limit on in-kind contributions like banners, balloons, and food, were the result of campaign finance laws and regulations. And a few, such as always notifying the Secret Service before firing a confetti cannon at a rally, were learned through trial and error. But no matter where a rule came from, it was up to the campaign and the Republican National Committee to implement it, and without a doubt the toughest rules to enforce were the ones that had to do with the potential political minefield known as introductions.

At every event, the president or the vice president has to be introduced before making his remarks. The easiest way to accomplish this is with the Voice of God, someone who stands offstage with a microphone and a good voice and says, "Ladies and gentlemen, the vice president of the United States," but usually the introduction is made by someone who is standing at the podium, and in front of the cameras—hence the rules.

If we'd wanted to, we could have had six or seven different people introduce Dad at every event during the 2004 campaign, but since there was limited time in the schedule and only so much that can be said about someone, even if he is the vice president of the United States, we tried to limit the number of introductions to two—one to introduce Dad, and one to introduce the person who was introducing Dad. If Mom was traveling with him, half of the problem was automatically solved. She would introduce him, and we'd ask a local VIP or elected official to introduce her. Otherwise priority would go to any VIPs in attendance. A John McCain or Rudy Giuliani would be at the top of the list, followed by the governor or senator of the state, and then members of the U.S. House of Representatives, local elected officials, and party leaders.

Once we knew who was giving the introductions, we needed to

know what they were going to say, so we'd ask for remarks to be submitted in writing several days before the event. Partly this was to ensure that they weren't saying anything inappropriate or that conflicted with administration policy, but primarily it was to make sure that the introduction wasn't too long. The White House set a firm one-minute limit on all introductions, and the campaign staff tried hard to enforce it, sometimes without much success. One U.S. senator, whose staff had submitted a very nice, very brief, very well-written introduction, got up on stage and decided to improvise. Instead of the prepared introduction, he gave a twelve-and-a-half-minute speech during which he not only introduced Dad, but also managed to give a good portion of Dad's speech—including most of the applause lines.

As the campaign progressed, some staff members noticed that the 2008 factor was beginning to crop up in the introductions. There seemed to be a direct correlation between the number of times someone introduced President Bush or Dad at an event, the length of that person's introductions, and the likelihood that the speaker was contemplating a run for president. One notable exception to this rule was John McCain. He always gave short, very thoughtful introductions even though everyone knew he had his eye on 2008.

The worst part about the rules regarding introductions was that when push came to shove, there really wasn't much the campaign could do to stop someone who didn't want to follow them. If a speaker went over the time limit or threw out his preapproved script, pulling him offstage or turning off his microphone might sound satisfying, but they really weren't viable options. Usually, the staff just had to smile, nod, and thank the speaker for making such a great introduction.

Fortunately, most of the elected officials and VIPs who traveled with my dad or spoke at campaign events were great to deal with.

They went out of their way to make the events a success, they were willing to do media interviews supporting the president's agenda, and they tried to respect my parents' rare moments of downtime. It was the exceptions, however, who kept us on our toes.

At the end of the 2000 campaign, Dad and Mom were scheduled to take a bus tour through a key battleground state. The state's Republican governor was traveling with them and he was supposed to meet my parents at their hotel before departing for the first event. On the morning of the tour, I got a phone call from one of the advance staff telling me that the governor had just arrived. He was a little early, so I asked the staffer to direct him to the coffee shop and said that I'd go tell Dad that he was downstairs. I figured Dad would want to go have a cup of coffee with him before we left on the bus tour.

The hotel was pretty modest even by campaign standards. My parents were staying in a very small room that had a couple of beds, a TV, and a very tiny bathroom. There wasn't even a closet, just a bar screwed to the wall with a dozen or so permanently attached hangers. It was Spartan, and not designed for entertaining guests, so I was very surprised when I walked in and found my parents sitting on one bed and the governor sitting on the other one. Mom and Dad had been getting ready to leave, when he unexpectedly knocked on their door. Both beds were covered with newspapers and luggage, and the room service tray leftover from breakfast— including the dirty dishes—was sitting on top of the television.

I found out later that Liz, who was traveling with us that week, had been there when the governor first showed up. She had gone to our parents' room to ask Mom a quick question, and she was still wearing her pajamas when she answered the knock on Mom and Dad's door and found the governor standing in the hallway. As the governor slipped past her into the room, the governor told Liz not to worry about being in her pajamas. He had daughters at home and totally understood what it was like to live in a house full of girls. He left out the fact that his daughters were all under the age of ten.

At that point, my parents didn't really have any choice but to offer the governor a cup of coffee from the lukewarm pot on the room service tray and a seat on one of the beds while they tried to make small talk. Apparently, the cramped quarters and dirty dishes didn't bother the governor, because when I showed up, he was offering his opinion regarding the state of the presidential race and his estimates regarding crowd size for the day's events. I quickly excused myself and went downstairs to try to find out how and why the governor had come up to the room when he was supposed to meet Mom and Dad in the coffee shop. The advance team told me that they'd tried to politely direct him to the coffee shop, but that he had walked right past them. He hadn't bothered to slow down or even make eye contact with them as he boarded the elevator. I decided that we were lucky that Liz was the only one still in her pajamas when he showed up.

The governor's visit illustrated an important lesson—no matter how many rules you may have, or how much planning you may do, you can't anticipate every possible situation that will arise on the campaign trail. No one would have ever thought to tell the advance staff what to do if a governor stormed my parents' hotel room. That's why some of the most valuable staffers on a campaign are the ones who can handle any situation that gets thrown at them.

There was a great group of such people on the finance staff, the department that raised the money to pay for everything from ads and polling to events, travel, yard signs, and bumper stickers. As well as managing the fundraising events, the finance staff tracked individual contributions, recruited people to serve as Rangers and Pioneers (individuals who committed to raise specific dollar amounts for the campaign), and ran direct mail operations. Overseeing the day-to-day operations was Jack Oliver, who had been the finance director in 2000 and is one of the best fundraisers I've ever met. He is high-energy, always worried about the bottom line, and is almost fanatical when it comes to making sure that the campaign's supporters know that their contributions are valued and appreciated and never taken for granted. Travis Thomas, Jack's deputy, is one of the nicest people I've ever worked with. He has a great sense of humor, is incredibly patient, and was always easy to deal with.

Jack and Travis's team could solve just about any problem—no matter how strange or untimely. They could handle people who showed up at a fundraiser dressed as polar bears (we thought they were probably protesting against drilling for oil in the Arctic National Wildlife Refuge, but they didn't have any signs so we had to guess about the issue). They knew just what to do when a fistfight broke out between the staffers of two VIPs during a photo op with contributors, and when a boat full of supporters got stranded in New York Harbor because the Secret Service wouldn't allow them to dock at the event site, they had just the right phone numbers programmed into their cell phones.

But some situations can baffle even the most capable campaign staffers. I once got a phone call from one of our advance men out on the road. Our conversation went something like this:

Advance Man: I need to let you know about a situation out here with the host's dog.

Me: Why? Did it bite someone?

Advance Man: No, it didn't bite anyone—it's dead.

Me: You killed the host's dog?

Advance Man: No . . . not me . . . well, technically speaking, one of the Secret Service agents kind of killed the host's dog.

Me: Kind of killed it? What did he do—shoot it?

Advance Man: No no—he didn't shoot it. It just sort of died. But I think it's OK, I mean the host doesn't seem upset about it or anything. I just wanted to give you a heads-up.

At this point, I asked the advance man to start at the beginning and tell me the whole story. Apparently, when the advance team, including a few Secret Service agents, showed up at the house for the first time, they were waiting outside for the host to show them around the property, when they saw a big old Newfoundland walking across the lawn. One of the agents called the dog over, knelt down, patted it on the head, and said something like, "Nice doggie." The dog wagged its tail, slobbered a little bit, and then fell over on its side—dead.

This of course caused great consternation among the advance team. They hadn't met the host yet, and now they were going to have to tell him that his dog had died while they were petting it. They were trying to decide between confessing and running away when the host walked out his front door, looked down at the scene on the lawn, and said, "Huh—dog died." He then pulled out his cell phone, dialed a number, and said, "Henry, dog died—better get the John Deere down here," hung up, and disappeared around the side of the house.

He reappeared a few moments later carrying some sort of black package under his arm—a body bag, as it turned out. The host rolled the dog into it and zipped it up—just as Henry pulled up with the backhoe. They dug a hole, put the body bag into the hole, then filled it in and tamped down the dirt. The host then gave the team a thorough tour of the property, during which he offered suggestions about where they ought to hold the photo op and the reception. He never mentioned the dog again, but the advance team and the agents found the whole thing pretty disturbing. I couldn't help but wonder how it was that he happened to have a body bag handy.

Fortunately, a lot of potential problems were headed off by the vetting process before they ever became an issue. Every venue that was used for a campaign event, every person who was onstage with the president, Mrs. Bush, Dad, or Mom, everyone who greeted them at the airport or at the venue, and anyone whose name appeared on an invitation as either a host or a committee member had to be vetted. Vetting involved searching the public record for any information that could be potentially embarrassing to the president or that might distract the media from covering the event's message. The campaign went through this labor-intensive process not because anyone really thought it mattered if we were planning on holding an event in a venue where there was also an art exhibit featuring anatomically correct chocolate sculptures of the human body, but because we knew the Democrats, at both the local and national levels, were vetting all of our events, hoping to find something, anything that they could feed to the media in an attempt to cause trouble and throw us off our message. It may sound slightly paranoid, but in the middle of a close presidential election, you have to do everything you can to stay on message, including not giving your opponent any possible ammunition to use against you. But not even the most thorough vetting and preparation can prevent every problem.

One of Dad's first nonfundraising events of the 2004 campaign was a speech contrasting President Bush's handling of the War on Terror with Senator Kerry's record on national security and defense issues. The speech would kick off a larger campaign program called "The Winning Weapons Tour," which was designed to highlight all of the weapons systems that had been instrumental in ensuring victory in Afghanistan and Iraq that Senator Kerry had voted against, or had proposed cutting or eliminating. It also marked a significant change in Dad's role from the 2000 campaign. Usually, vice presidential candidates are expected to be hatchet men, to take on the opposition's record and lead the attack. That way the presidential candidate can remain presidential. In 2000, however, both Dad and Governor Bush kept a positive tone throughout the campaign. Sure, there was some give and take and a few sharp one-liners, but for the most part the campaign stayed relatively positive.

But in 2004, one of Dad's main responsibilities was to point out the weaknesses in Senator Kerry's record, particularly on issues of national security and defense, which allowed the president to stay above the fray and to maintain his role as commander-in-chief— an incredibly important consideration for a campaign taking place during wartime. It was a more traditional role for the running mate, and it meant that Dad's speeches were much more aggressive and hard-hitting than they'd been during the first campaign.

Because this would be a major speech, one that the campaign hoped would drive a significant amount of media coverage, we wanted to hold it in a venue that had some symbolic significance. No one thought that a convention hall or a hotel ballroom would be special enough. Less than a week before the scheduled date for the speech, Ken Mehlman suggested Westminster College in Fulton, Missouri. It had been the site of Winston Churchill's famous "Iron Curtain" speech in 1946, in which he warned the West about Soviet expansion and cautioned against military weakness in the face of it. Over the years, the college has also hosted important speeches by Ronald Reagan, Margaret Thatcher, Lech Walesa, and Mikhail Gorbachev. It would be a great setting for Dad.

Following campaign rules, we submitted the school for vetting, and to no one's surprise it came back clean. Ken called Fletcher Lamkin, the school's president and a former West Point dean, asked if we could hold an event at the college, and clearly explained what would be in Dad's speech. No one wanted the school's administration to be caught off-guard, so when Kara Ahern, who was in charge of the event, followed up Ken's phone call, she also clearly explained the nature of the speech, telling President Lamkin, as Ken had, that it would be a campaign speech and that while most of it would be about President Bush's record, a significant portion would frankly critique Senator Kerry's record. President Lamkin said that the school looked forward to hosting my father.

The speech was great. Dad did an outstanding job of laying out the case for the president and against Senator Kerry. He talked about the president's actions following the attacks of September 11, the success of coalition troops in Afghanistan and Iraq, and how America's steady leadership had contributed to Libya's decision to voluntarily dismantle and disclose all of its WMD programs. He went on to talk about Senator Kerry's record of inconsistency, including his ever-changing position on Saddam Hussein and the war in Iraq; his claim that intelligence and law enforcement should be the primary weapons against terrorism (even though his record showed that he repeatedly tried to cut the intelligence budget); and Senator Kerry's now-famous answer to a question about a proposed $87-billion supplemental appropriation for troops fighting in Iraq and Afghanistan: "I actually did vote for the $87 billion before I voted against it."

Dad was repeatedly interrupted by applause. In the middle of the speech, there was even a standing ovation, and Fletcher Lamkin, seated onstage, was as enthusiastic as everyone else. Not surprisingly, given his military background, he seemed particularly receptive to the idea that a commander-in-chief ought fully to support our troops. When the speech was over, President Lamkin graciously thanked my father for visiting Westminster College, and was friendly and courteous to my parents throughout their time on campus.

Then, a few hours later, he sent out an email addressed to all faculty, staff, and students at Westminster College. It expressed dismay at my dad's speech: "Frankly, I must admit that I was surprised and disappointed that Mr. Cheney chose to step off the high ground and resort to Kerry-bashing for a large portion of his speech." He went on to claim that the school had been told that Dad's speech would be only about foreign policy, including the situation in Iraq. Given that President Lamkin had in fact been told several times that it would be a hard-hitting political/campaign speech contrasting the records of President Bush and Senator Kerry, everyone at the campaign was more than a little surprised when reporters started calling and asking about the email.

While I don't know for sure why President Lamkin sent out the email, an explanation I heard later made some sense: that Lamkin had received complaints from some of his faculty about the partisan tone of Dad's speech (kind of amazing how college faculty never complain about liberal speakers who express a partisan point of view) and that he sent out the email to placate them. Of course, once the email went out to everyone at Westminster College, it wasn't long before the AP, the *New York Times*, CNN, and every other media outlet had it.

As annoyed as I was, President Lamkin's email ultimately played in our favor. Because of it, Dad's speech got more coverage than it would have without the controversy. Throughout the day, the cable news channels replayed the excerpts in which Dad talked about Senator Kerry's record. The speech also threw the Kerry campaign off-message. The senator was on a bus tour through Ohio to talk about jobs, but instead he spent time attacking Dad's draft deferments and the president's service in the National Guard. While I don't particularly enjoy listening to people attack my father, any time the opposition's presidential nominee goes after your vice presidential candidate, it's a good thing. It lessens the stature of the candidate making the attack, and it allows your presidential candidate to stay above it all. Senator Kerry himself pumped more life into the story a few days later when he went to Westminster College to deliver his own foreign policy speech. It was weak and vague, as his speeches on Iraq usually were. And the news coverage of it invariably included clips of Dad's—thereby increasing the total amount of coverage of Dad talking about Senator Kerry's record.

While the whole episode was ultimately a net gain for the Bush-Cheney campaign, no one wanted to go through it again, so we decided that for future campaign events, we would content ourselves with places that we could rent. Convention centers, airport hangars, and county fairgrounds might not offer the same level of symbolism as Westminster College, but they were easier to control, and offered significantly less risk, always a good idea.

My mom once offered this observation about child raising: You can never make the list of rules long enough. You can say "Don't run with scissors," and "Don't cross the street without looking both ways," but there will always be something that's not on the list, like "Don't stick an eraser up your nose." (I won't say who in our family tried that one out.)

Campaigns are a lot like that. No matter how long the list of rules, the unexpected will happen, whether it's a host's pet picking a particularly inopportune moment to expire or a college president conveniently rewriting the history of an event after the fact.

CHAPTER 12

SLOTUS

Most people refer to them as Secret Service code names, but technically they're White House Communications Agency (WHCA) call signs. Because few people ever get one, they are one of the most coveted status symbols in Washington, D.C. They are assigned to Secret Service protectees, cabinet members, key White House staffers, and individuals who are in the line of presidential succession, like the Speaker of the House of Representatives.

In the case of cabinet secretaries, the call sign stays the same regardless of who occupies the office. The treasury secretary is always "Fencing Master," the secretary of education is "Fraction," and "Fist Fight" is the secretary of health and human services. But for the two highest offices, the call signs are unique. Each new president and vice president gets a call sign that is assigned just to them.

Every four years, as soon as a presidential or vice presidential candidate picks up Secret Service protection, WHCA assigns that candidate a letter in the alphabet. Exactly how the letter is chosen is a mystery. Some people claim that it is randomly generated by a computer, others insist that it's picked out of a hat during some sort of elaborate secret ritual. However it happens, once the letter is selected, WHCA draws up a list of suggested call signs for the candidate starting with that letter, which is also used for the call signs of everyone in the candidate's family. In our family, all the call signs start with the letter A.

Because the call signs for the president, the vice president, and their families are assigned to the individual rather than the office, they often reflect a personal characteristic or trait. Former president Jimmy Carter, a born-again Christian, is "Deacon." Former President Ronald Reagan, an avid horseman, was "Rawhide." Dad, a diehard fly fisherman is "Angler," while Mom, a successful writer, is "Author." Because I love the mountains and enjoy snowboarding and mountain biking, my call sign is "Alpine."

The number of people with a call sign is relatively small, roughly thirty or so in any given administration, but there is an even smaller and more exclusive group in the hierarchy of Washington, D.C., politics—the people who are referred to by an acronym or an abbreviation of their title. Some of these, like POTUS (President of the United States) and VPOTUS (Vice President of the United States) are fairly well known. Others, like SECDEF (Secretary of Defense) are rarely recognized by people outside the beltway. I'm not sure why it is, but something about the abbreviations and acronyms exudes an air of power and confidence, or in the case of FLOTUS (First Lady of the United States), an air of grace. They all just sound kind of cool—all of them, that is, except the one given to the wife of the vice president, SLOTUS (Second Lady of the United States).

The first time anyone in my family heard the term SLOTUS was at the inauguration in 2001. It was the night after the swearing-in, and the Cheney family was making the tour of all the inaugural balls. We were standing backstage at the Texas-Wyoming ball while the advance team explained the program. They had set up a diagram showing where everyone was supposed to stand onstage. My brother-in-law, Phil, studied the diagram for a minute and then asked, "What's a SLOTUS?" I thought it sounded vaguely medical (Jack can't play in the game tonight—he pulled his SLOTUS), but the advance team explained that it stood for Second Lady of the United States, prompting my mother to put her face in her hands and moan in mock despair, "Oh, no, it's me!" Later she observed that it sounded like something out of a Faulkner novel, where the creepy people have names like "Flem Snopes."

The term does raise a larger question: What do you call the wife of the vice president? I've heard my mom introduced as "The Second Lady," "The Second First Lady," and "The Vice First Lady." I've heard that Tipper Gore was once introduced to an audience as "The First Lady of Vice." It's no wonder that my mom usually prefers to be introduced as "Lynne Cheney" or "Mrs. Cheney."

My niece Elizabeth came up with the best title for Mom. She was four and Liz and Phil had taken her and her sisters out to Northern California to visit Phil's parents. Understanding that all children like to hear stories about adults making mistakes, Liz told Elizabeth about the time when we were little and my mom took us to San Francisco to visit some friends. While she was driving us across the Bay Bridge, she managed to do exactly what you shouldn't do: She ran out of gas. Elizabeth loved the story, but she was a little confused because Liz had been referring to Mom as "Grandma" and Phil's mom was also known as Grandma. "You mean Grandma Julie?" she asked. Liz said no, it was "Grandma Lynne." This didn't clarify much since the girls never use my mom's first name, but after a few seconds, Elizabeth got it. "Oh," she said, "you mean the Grandma of the United States," which is probably one of the best titles that anyone has ever been given.

The wife of the vice president usually keeps a much lower profile than the first lady, but she still has quite a few official obligations, most of which my mother really enjoys. She loves the bands and pageantry that accompany events like the official arrivals of foreign dignitaries at the White House. One of her favorite events is putting the star on top of the National Christmas Tree every year, primarily because she gets to take the grandkids up in the crane with her. Barbara Bush and her grandchildren liked this job so much during the eight years she was second lady that she continued to do it during her time in the White House.

But not all second lady assignments are that great—at least for my mom. Every year, one of the Washington wives' clubs hosts a luncheon. The first lady, the wife of the vice president, and all the wives of the cabinet officers are not only expected to attend, but they have to enter the event by way of an elevated runway, similar to what you see at fashion shows, but a lot longer. Each woman walks out on the arm of a military aide and is introduced as "the wife of the secretary of the treasury," "the wife of the secretary of state," "the wife of the vice president of the United States." I've heard my mother say how much she likes many of the women in this club, but, boy, does she hate the retrograde runway "wife of" routine. When she managed to miss the luncheon one spring, she heard about her absence from various club members for the rest of the year. Their spouses even complained to my dad. So, now my mom always goes. I've heard Hillary Clinton once tried to miss the luncheon as well, but eventually she also gave in.

My mom has never been a stereotypical political wife. She has a Ph.D. in English and has taught at a number of colleges and universities. Ronald Reagan appointed her chairman of the National Endowment of the Humanities, a position she held throughout George H. W. Bush's administration. She was one of the hosts of *Crossfire Sunday* on CNN during the 1990s, where her penchant for speaking her mind won her a real following. Even after *Cross-fire* went off the air, people would still come up to me and say how much they wished Mom would go back on the program. She's also served on numerous corporate boards, including Lockheed-Martin and Reader's Digest. She is now a senior fellow at the American Enterprise Institute, a Washington think tank, and a published author, which makes her the first wife of a president or vice president to continue working while her husband is in office.

Mom's role in the campaign changed greatly between 2000 and 2004. In 2000, she traveled with Dad about half the time and spent the rest campaigning on her own or as part of a "W Stands for Women" tour, which targeted women in battleground states. Condoleeza Rice, Barbara Bush, and Mom would speak to audiences and give media interviews encouraging women to vote for George W. Bush. Mom usually tried to arrange her schedule so that she traveled only for a day or two on her own before meeting up with Dad. After spending time on the road, she always looked forward to getting back on the campaign plane. It might creak and groan when it landed, but it was the center of our campaign universe, the place where you could get the latest polls and the latest word on what was happening. My mom dubbed it "the Mothership."

In 2004, with the exception of a handful of events, Mom always traveled with Dad, primarily because after forty years of marriage, they are both happier when they are together. She is his most trusted advisor and his best friend. When she was with him, his speeches were sharper, his mood was more upbeat, and his events were always better.

In her introductions of him, she'd tell stories about their growing up together in Casper, Wyoming, like the one about the red dress her grandmother, who did alterations at the H & G Drycleaners in Casper, had made her. It was red crinoline and strapless, and she wore it on her first date with my father. "I think it was the reason I got a second date," she would say. Then Dad would come to the podium, shake his head, and say, "It was a great dress." Crowds loved hearing personal stories about my parents, and they would get Dad's speeches off to a great start.

The other reason Mom didn't travel much on her own in 2004 was simply that it cost too much. Due to a combination of government regulations, campaign finance laws, and campaign guidelines, it was considerably more expensive to send my mom to an event than it was to send my dad, the president, or Mrs. Bush. POTUS, VPOTUS, and FLOTUS all travel on military aircraft, but SLOTUS doesn't, so if Mom needed to get to Oconomowoc, Wisconsin, or Malvern, Pennsylvania, in a timely fashion, the campaign had to find a plane for her. According to campaign finance laws, the campaign could use corporate airplanes so long as we reimbursed the owners for the cost of a first-class ticket, which is much less than the cost of chartering a plane, and that's how she flew around the country in 2000. But in 2004, she was the wife of the vice president, so in order to avoid any perception of impropriety, it was determined that she wouldn't travel on any plane owned by an individual or a corporation. That basically meant that we couldn't use anything but an expensive charter. In addition, the federal government has some strange rules governing how much it can reimburse a campaign whenever a federal employee, such as a Secret Service agent, flies on a chartered aircraft. The effect of all this was that, on average, it cost the campaign two to three times more to send my mom to an event on her own than it did to send my dad or the president.

So having Mom and Dad travel together made them happier, saved the campaign money, and gave Dad the benefit of her input and ideas. One of her best ideas came in the final days of the campaign. We had just finished a rally in International Falls, Minnesota, when my mom walked into the staff office and asked if we could go to Hawaii.

A couple of public polls in the last weeks of the campaign showed that President Bush was trailing Senator Kerry by only a couple of points in what is traditionally a very safe Democratic state. No one really gave us much of a chance to win there, but everyone at the White House and the campaign thought Mom had a great idea. If Dad did an event in Honolulu, it would show that we were on offense, taking no vote for granted and going after traditional Democratic strongholds. It would get us several days' worth of media buzz about how aggressive the Bush-Cheney campaign was being in the final days, and seeing us challenging the Kerry-Edwards campaign's claim to Hawaii's electoral votes would help fire up our supporters across the country.

I immediately got to work with the advance team and Elizabeth Kleppe, the director of vice presidential scheduling at the White House, to see if it was possible to fly all the way to Honolulu and back without canceling any of the events that were already scheduled. It turned out that it could be done, but we would have to fly all night, hold a rally on Halloween night at ten o'clock in Honolulu, and then immediately fly to Colorado to make our scheduled rally in Colorado Springs the next morning. It would be a very long and ugly day, but we could do it.

The political staff assured me that they could get a big crowd for the rally, and they did. Ten thousand people jammed into the Honolulu Convention Center for what was a truly unique political event. There were the usual local political VIPs, but most of them were wearing leis and Hawaiian shirts, and the entertainment consisted of hula dancers and fire twirlers instead of the standard high school marching band.

The handful of events Mom did on her own in 2004 were ones

that campaign leadership or the political office at the White House deemed high priorities: fundraisers for targeted congressional candidates and battleground state parties as well as events aimed at key demographic groups like business owners, parents, or women.

In May 2004, I received an invitation for my mom to speak at the national convention of Women in Public Policy, a group of female entrepreneurs. I did some checking on the group and asked Mom if she wanted to go. She said no. Dad was scheduled to travel to Michigan and Iowa that week, and she wanted to go with him, so I declined the invitation on her behalf.

Less than a day later, I received phone calls and emails from Ken Mehlman; Maria Cino, deputy chairman of the Republican National Committee; Jafar Karim, head of coalitions for the Bush-Cheney campaign; and Cathy Gillespie, the director of the "W Stands for Women" program, who all wanted Mom to reconsider her decision. It turned out that Women in Public Policy had requested a representative from both the Bush-Cheney and the Kerry campaigns, and Teresa Heinz Kerry had already committed to speak. Ken Mehlman and the others were concerned that if we didn't send a high-profile representative, it might reflect negatively on our campaign and offend the organization's members. Everyone agreed that my mom was the best choice to serve as our representative, so I asked her to reconsider. She agreed.

When I called the group to let them know that Mom would be attending, they told me that Mrs. Kerry wanted to do something more interactive than give a set speech, so she was going to hold a town hall meeting and take questions from the audience. I thought it would be weird if Mom read from a prepared text after Mrs. Kerry held a town hall. Mom agreed that a town hall would be a lot more interesting, and suggested that she and Mrs. Kerry could hold a joint town hall. I thought it was a great idea, and the group loved it as well. They said they would check with the Kerry campaign and let us know.

Mom is a great public speaker, knows the issues better than almost anyone, and is incredibly good at staying on message. I didn't think there was any way the Kerry campaign would allow Mrs. Kerry to go head-to-head with her. With her experience on *Crossfire* and on the campaign trail, I knew she would be really good, and I almost didn't believe it when Terry Neese from Women in Public Policy called back and said that Mrs. Kerry had agreed to a joint event.

I quickly pulled together Mom's wish list regarding format, time limits, and topics and turned it over to Kara Ahern, my deputy and the person responsible for working out the logistics. I also recruited Liz and Mary Matalin to help prep Mom.

A few days before the event, Kara told me that we had gotten everything we wanted in terms of format and timing. She also told me that she just found out that Terry McAuliffe, the chairman of the Democratic National Committee, had apparently been negotiating on behalf of Mrs. Kerry. I immediately wondered why Terry McAuliffe would be involved. Admittedly, the event had the potential to generate a good deal of press, but it seemed odd that the chairman of the Democratic National Committee would be involved in working out small details such as who speaks first and if the audience members have to submit their questions in writing. The only thing I could figure out was that the Kerry campaign was probably worried about what might happen at the event, and they'd asked Terry McAuliffe to try to keep it from becoming a complete disaster.

Once all of the details were locked in, I emailed Ken Mehlman, Maria Cino, Cathy Gillespie, and everyone else who had told me how important it was for my mom to do this event, to let them know that it was going to be a joint town hall with Mrs. Kerry. I believe I also told them that my mom was going to kick Teresa Heinz Kerry's butt.

Shortly after I hit the send button, Michael Napolitano, Ken Mehlman's assistant, came running into my office and said, "You are being summoned to the conference room like I have never seen anyone summoned before." I knew this couldn't possibly be good news, but also had no idea what I might have done to warrant such a summons.

I walked into the conference room to find Karl Rove; Ken Mehlman; Mark Wallace, Bush-Cheney deputy campaign manager; Nicolle Devenish, Bush-Cheney communications director; Ed Gillespie, RNC chairman; Dan Bartlett, White House communications director—everybody who was anybody, in other words. Karen Hughes was on a speaker phone from her home in Austin. Karl pulled out the chair next to his, patted the seat, and said, "Mary, there you are. Come sit by me." Not seeing that I really had any choice in the matter, I sat. He asked me to tell him about the debate I had arranged between my mom and Mrs. Kerry. I explained that it wasn't really a debate, that it was a joint town hall, that we'd agreed on a format, that Mary Matalin and Liz were working with the policy shop to pull together prep materials for Mom, and that Women in Public Policy would be sending out a press release announcing the event by the close of business.

From the reaction I got, you would have thought that I'd just announced that a biblical plague was about to be visited upon the face of the earth. Everyone started talking at once, so I couldn't quite make out what they were saying, but there was much gnashing of teeth, rending of hair, and moaning and wailing with palms toward heaven. The consensus seemed to be that Mom couldn't possibly take part in the event and that we needed to cancel it before the organization sent out the press release. The group had several concerns, but the main one seemed to be that Mom would be setting a precedent for the president. If she took part in the joint town hall, the Kerry campaign could demand that the president start holding regular debates with Senator Kerry. At the very least, they argued, we would face several weeks of news stories about the president's ducking John Kerry.

None of this made sense to me. I said there was a big difference between Lynne Cheney and Teresa Heinz Kerry holding a joint town hall and the president and Senator Kerry holding a series of formal debates. The president is the leader of the free world, busy governing the country and fighting the War on Terror. My mom isn't. There was no precedent for a sitting president debating his opponent this early in the campaign—months before the national conventions, and long before any of the dates proposed by the Commission on Presidential Debates. No one, except possibly the Kerry campaign, would demand, or expect, the president to start debating until the fall simply because my mom was sharing a stage with Mrs. Kerry.

I also pointed out that the only reason Mom was taking part in the event was that several of the people in that very room had told me she had to, and begged me to convince her to go. Now that she'd agreed, I didn't see how we could cancel it without talking to her first. At that point, Ken suggested we call her on the spot.

I imagined my mom's response to a semihysterical group call-ing her and demanding that she cancel something that she hadn't wanted to do in the first place, and had agreed to do only after being begged—by some of the very people who were now so spun-up about it. I said I'd call her from my office, which I did. Only mildly irritated, she said sure, go ahead, pull the plug on the joint town hall, but what, she wanted to know, was going on at the campaign? I confessed that I was as mystified as she was. I was just glad I hadn't told anybody about Terry McAuliffe. That would have just further convinced the group in the conference room that the Women in Public Policy event was part of some sort of vast Democratic conspiracy.

I will always think of that day as the day that a great political event met its demise. I would have loved to have seen my mom onstage with Teresa Heinz Kerry. But I also remember it as the day that I saved Ken Mehlman's life. When I think of what Mom's reaction would have been if I'd let him and a group of overexcited people ambush her on a speakerphone, I think that he ought to be very, very grateful to me.

CHAPTER 13

Freedom Means Freedom
for Everyone

On January 20, 2004, in his State of the Union address, President Bush declared, "Our nation must defend the sanctity of marriage." His statement didn't come as a surprise. The Federal Marriage Amendment had been a topic of discussion in strategy sessions and senior staff meetings at the campaign for several weeks, ever since the Supreme Judicial Court of Massachusetts had ruled that barring same-sex couples from marrying was a violation of the Massachusetts Constitution. Radio call-in shows and television news programs were spending a lot of time on the debate over same-sex marriage, and everyone assumed that the president would address the issue in the State of the Union.

I'd been scheduled to sit in the House Gallery during the president's address, but after seeing an advance copy of the speech, I changed my plans. I didn't want to be there when the members of the House and Senate and all of the invited guests applauded the president's declaration. I sure wasn't going to stand up and cheer. And, even though President Bush stopped short of offering an outright endorsement of the Federal Marriage Amendment in the State of the Union, I knew that it was only a matter of time before he did so, and I also knew that I needed to decide if I could continue working for the re-election of a president who wanted to write discrimination into the Constitution of the United States. It wasn't an easy decision for me to make, and in the days that followed I came very close to quitting my job as director of VP Operations for the Bush-Cheney '04 campaign. I seriously considered packing up my office and heading home to Colorado.

A few people at the campaign tried to make me feel better by telling me that the Federal Marriage Amendment really wasn't a big deal. They pointed out that same-sex marriage had never been recognized in the United States and that no politician with a reasonable chance of becoming president had ever spoken out on behalf of it. The Defense of Marriage Act, signed by President Clinton in 1996, already defined marriage at the federal level as being between a man and a woman and allowed individual states to refuse to recognize same-sex marriages performed in other states. The Federal Marriage Amendment wouldn't change anything, they said. It would just reinforce the status quo. I explained to them that, from my perspective, it would change everything.

There's a historical analogy I like to use. The Fourteenth Amendment, which was introduced in 1866 and ratified in 1868, defined all persons born or naturalized in the United States as citizens, gave federal protection to individual rights, and established the idea of "equal protection." It also said that the number of representatives apportioned to a state would be based upon the number of male citizens allowed to vote in that state. Prior to this, the word *male* did not appear in the Constitution, meaning that although women had few rights in the society at the time, they were not explicitly denied them in the Constitution. Women could look to our founding document as one that included them, even if society itself

did not, and they could hope that one day society would understand that equality is a concept applicable to all human beings. But
when the word *male* was written into the Constitution, the document became specifically exclusionary, and the women who had
spent years working for suffrage and other rights were angered and
dismayed. As they said in 1866 in the Resolutions of the Equal
Rights convention in Syracuse, New York, "The introduction of the
word 'male' . . . is a gross affront to women everywhere."

In these early years of the twenty-first century, society may not
recognize gays and lesbians as deserving of the same rights and
protections as other citizens, but nowhere in the Constitution are
they specifically excluded from having them. The Federal Marriage
Amendment would change that. It would deny same-sex couples
the hope that their relationships might one day receive the same
recognition, rights, and protections that married couples take
for granted every day, and it would write discrimination into the
Constitution, our nation's most important and influential document. It is fundamentally wrong—and a gross affront to gays and
lesbians everywhere.

The day after the president's State of the Union speech, I spent
a long time on the phone talking to Heather, who was just as
troubled as I was. I told her I wasn't sure what I was going to do,
quit or stay on the campaign. Completely understanding as always,
she told me, "Only you can decide what is right for you to do—
come home or stay there—just know I love you and will support
whatever you decide."

Late that afternoon, I called Dad and told him that I needed to
talk. He asked me to come to his office at the White House. I also
called my mom, and when I told her I was going over to the White
House, she said she'd meet me there. Liz, who was downtown,
came as well. She was wearing jeans, which are forbidden in the
White House, but that didn't stop her. She walked right into the

West Wing anyway. The four of us sat around my dad's desk, with me doing most of the talking, or venting, I guess you'd call it, and Mom, Dad, and Liz offering their support. They told me in as many ways as they could that they would totally understand if I felt that I had to quit. But they also made clear that I was filling an important job for Dad and for our whole family at the campaign and that they wanted me to stay. At a time when I was hurt, angry, and exhausted from not having slept the night before, it was nice to hear my parents and Liz say what complete faith and trust they had in me and to talk about how much they valued the job I had been doing.

They also made it clear that they wanted me to stay because they didn't want me to be driven away by a policy position with which we all disagreed. During the 2000 vice presidential debate, Dad had said that he thought marriage and legal recognition of relationships was a matter for individual states to decide. He always acknowledged that President Bush ultimately sets policy for the administration, but he also made it clear that he personally did not support the Federal Marriage Amendment.

After we talked for a couple of hours, Dad and I had to leave for a fundraiser in New York. We had said pretty much everything there was to say, but I still wasn't sure what I was going to do. Mom hadn't been scheduled to go to New York, but at the last minute she decided she would come with us, and I appreciated her company. The event was held in a low-ceilinged apartment that someone said had once belonged to Katie Couric, and while Dad was taking pictures with various donors, Mom and I sat across from each other on a pair of twin beds in one of the apartment's bedrooms. She was worried about me, she said. She wanted me to stay on the campaign, but not as much as she wanted me to be happy. "If you feel like you have to leave," she said, "then that's the right thing to do."

I'm not sure when exactly I decided to stay, but by the time President Bush stood up in front of the White House Press Corps on

February 24, 2004, and said, "Today I call upon the Congress to promptly pass, and to send to the states for ratification, an amendment to our Constitution defining and protecting marriage as a union of man and woman as husband and wife," I knew that no matter how much I disagreed with him on this issue, I was going to see the campaign through to Election Day.

The most important reason was my father. I love my dad. He is a man of intelligence, integrity, wisdom, and character. I was honored when he asked me to oversee his campaign operation and had promised him that I would do the job to the best of my ability. When I made that promise back in September 2002, I didn't know that President Bush would endorse a constitutional amendment banning same-sex marriage, but his doing so didn't change the fact that I had made the commitment and, more important, that I strongly believed in my father.

It also helped that I only heard one high-ranking Republican strategist complain that the campaign needed to "fix" Dad's position on the marriage amendment to bring it back in line with the president's. Certainly, a few right-wing interest groups issued statements complaining about Dad's position, but I never heard anyone from the White House or the campaign criticize his statements. While not everyone at the campaign or in the White House agreed with Dad's position, most of them understood that there were people, including a lot of Republicans, who weren't in favor of amending the Constitution, and they respected those differences of opinion. One of those people was President Bush.

Dad called me the day that the president announced his support of the Federal Marriage Amendment to let me know that the president had told him that he would understand if I wanted to issue a public statement expressing my opposition to it. While I appreciated the gesture, I didn't think it was appropriate for me as a campaign staffer to issue a statement. The only thing it would have accomplished would have been to turn me and my sexual orientation into a prime-time campaign issue, something I was very much trying to avoid—as it turns out, without much success.

There was one other reason why I decided to stay on the campaign and that was because I believed that despite endorsing the Federal Marriage Amendment, George W. Bush was still the best candidate to lead the United States at this point in our history. Obviously, the amendment was an incredibly personal issue for me, and I completely disagreed with the president's position, but, in the election of 2004, I didn't have the luxury of voting on that issue alone.

The biggest challenge facing the country was the War on Terror. Given that the primary responsibility of the president of the United States is to serve as commander-in-chief, and given that we live in a world where terrorists and the countries that support them would love nothing more than to attack this nation, it seemed pretty clear that we needed to elect the candidate who would do the best job of defending and protecting this country, her people, and her interests. In 2004, there was no question that that candidate was George W. Bush.

I don't need to rehash all of Senator Kerry's failings in the area of national security. I think everyone was well aware of them by the end of the campaign. Even his friends had to be appalled at his shifts and changes. He left no clear idea of where he stood— indeed, leaving everything a little fuzzy sometimes seemed to be his goal. War requires a determined leader, which Senator Kerry gave no hint of being, and which George Bush had exhibited he was.

And it's important to note that the choice in 2004 wasn't exactly between someone who was solid on gay and lesbian issues and someone who was the kind of strong leader we needed. When it seemed like the politically advantageous thing to do, Senator Kerry waffled on a constitutional amendment banning gay marriage in Massachusetts, changing his position from strong opposition to conditional support. But even if he'd been perfect on gay and lesbian issues, that wouldn't have been enough for me. In the end, we have to preserve this country where we can debate subjects like gay marriage and work to achieve a society where, as my dad said in 2000, "freedom means freedom for everyone." And we are going to be hard put to do that without purposeful, determined leaders.

Those were my thoughts as I decided to stay. It still gave me a knot in the pit of my stomach to think of my candidate for president endorsing the Federal Marriage Amendment, but it helped that in the days and weeks afterward, many campaign staffers, including members of the senior staff, came into my office, shut the door, and told me that they disagreed with the president on this issue. Usually the staffer had a family member or a close friend who was gay, or had lived in a large urban area with a significant gay population and knew lots of gay people. They were troubled by the amendment. It was unfair, it was discriminatory, it would hurt people they knew and cared about, and it didn't belong in the Constitution of the United States. They disagreed with the president, but they also knew it was important that he be re-elected.

Having all of these young campaign staffers tell me that the Federal Marriage Amendment was wrong and discriminatory reinforced my belief that same-sex marriage isn't a Republican or Democratic issue as much as it is a generational one. Public opinion polls show that one of the key indicators of a person's opinion regarding same-sex marriage is age. Younger voters are much more likely than older voters to favor legalizing same-sex marriage. Fairly typical are the results from an ABC News poll taken immediately following the President's 2004 State of the Union address in which 55 percent of those under the age of thirty favored legalizing same-sex marriage while only 21 percent of those over the age of sixty-five expressed the same view.

When all ages were polled, legalizing same-sex marriage had only minority support (37 percent for legalizing it, 55 percent opposed), so opposition to it still offers some political advantage, but that will change as younger voters displace older ones. And while the Federal Marriage Amendment no doubt helped many Republican candidates in 2004 and may continue to help them in the next few elections, ultimately, I believe, candidates who support discrimination and advocate amending the Constitution will face an electorate that sees their views as prejudiced and intolerant.

In 1967, the U.S. Supreme Court handed down its landmark decision in *Loving* v. *Virginia,* which declared that miscegenation laws banning interracial marriage were unconstitutional. It was an incredibly unpopular decision. A Gallup poll taken at the time showed that 72 percent of the public opposed the idea of interracial marriage. Forty years later, no serious candidate for public office would dream of advocating a ban on interracial marriage, and any candidate who dared take such a position would be driven from the race by a firestorm of public opinion.

It won't take forty years for opposition to same-sex marriage to dissipate, and support for a constitutional amendment banning it will prove to have an even shorter half-life. If the Republican Party fails to come around on this issue, I believe it will find itself on the wrong side of history and on a sharp decline into irrelevance.

Of all the personal stories I heard from people during the debate over the Federal Marriage Amendment, there is one in particular that stands out. Shortly after President Bush announced his support for the Federal Marriage Amendment, I got a call from one of his longtime supporters who had recently come to terms with the fact that he is gay.

He called me because a handful of gay activists had started an outing campaign and they were targeting gay people who supported the president or who worked at the campaign, the White House, or the Republican National Committee. This man called me because he thought there was a very good chance that he would be next. He wasn't ashamed or conflicted about being gay, but he was worried that his supervisor might have a problem with it, and he wanted to know if I had any advice for him.

On the theory that it's always better to deliver the news yourself rather than allow your boss to be surprised, I told him that if he really thought he was about to be outed, he owed it to his supervisor to tell him. I couldn't guarantee how his supervisor would react, but figured it would undoubtedly be worse if he found out from a reporter. I felt very sorry for the guy. He was in a horrible position without any good options. He hadn't been the one to endorse the Federal Marriage Amendment, and hadn't even been involved in the policy decision, but because of his sexual orientation, he was being targeted for outing and now he feared for his job.

The situation nagged at me for the rest of the day, and when I saw my dad later that evening, I mentioned it to him. Without divulging any names, I told him about the phone call and about how bad I felt for this man who had been nothing but loyal to the president, but who was now worried about his job and his future.

Dad listened to the whole story and then said, "That's just unacceptable. I want you to go back and tell this person that if anyone—I don't care who it is—if anyone gives him any trouble, he is to come see me and I'll take care of it." The next morning I called the man back and told him word for word what Dad had said, relieving him, I think, of at least some of his worries.

The phone call and the conversation with my dad reinforced my decision to stay on the campaign. I would never agree with the president's endorsement of a constitutional amendment banning gay marriage, but I'd made a commitment to the campaign and to my family, and I knew how crucial it was to win this election. Most important, I was working for a candidate I knew I could count on, a man I could support without reservation. I was working for my dad.

CHAPTER 14

New York

Every four years, political reporters spend a great deal of time analyzing the "gender gap"—the fact that women historically favor Democratic candidates while men tend to support Republicans. In 2004, closing the gender gap was an important objective for the Bush-Cheney campaign, and one that paid off on election night. In 2000, according to the exit polls, George W. Bush received 43 percent of the votes cast by women. By 2004, that number had grown to 48 percent. But while the Bush-Cheney campaign did a great job of closing the gender gap in 2004, and even managed to make inroads with other traditional Democratic constituencies like Hispanics, there was one demographic gap that we couldn't close—the celebrity gap.

The Bush-Cheney campaign wasn't the first Republican presidential campaign to suffer from the celebrity gap. It's been a constant feature of every presidential election of the last forty years. Richard Nixon demolished George McGovern in the 1972 election, even though most of Hollywood backed Senator McGovern. Stars such as Warren Beatty, Paul Newman, and Shirley MacLaine campaigned on behalf of McGovern, while the Nixon campaign received the backing of celebrities such as Ruta Lee, the actress and star of such movies as *The Doomsday Machine* and *Bullets for a Badman.*

In 2000, Ben Affleck, Martin Sheen, Alfre Woodard, and Jon Bon Jovi hit the campaign trail on behalf of Vice President Gore. Director Robert Altman and musician Eddie Vedder both went so far as to proclaim that they'd leave the country if George W. Bush won the election (neither actually did). And, in a moment of particularly high-minded political oratory, Cher publicly wondered if all Bush supporters had "lost their f——king minds."

At the rally introducing Senator Joe Lieberman as the Democratic vice presidential nominee, the warmup act was the singer Jewel, whose records were selling by the millions. That same day, my parents attended a fundraiser in California that featured Debbie Boone singing the song "You Light Up My Life." While everyone certainly appreciated Ms. Boone's willingness to perform at the event, I learned later that she was there not because she necessarily supported Governor Bush. She'd agreed to perform because she was a close friend of the family who hosted the fundraiser.

One reason campaigns court celebrities is that they're an easy way to help build a crowd. In 2004, the Kerry campaign held a rally in Madison, Wisconsin, that drew eighty thousand people, most of whom came not to see John Kerry, but to catch a glimpse of his special guest, Bruce Springsteen. It's not unusual for Democratic presidential candidates to have famous entertainers at almost every big event, particularly in the last days leading up to an election. Republicans, on the other hand, have to be more strategic in their use of celebrity endorsements. When there aren't a lot of entertainers who are eager to campaign on your behalf, you have to make sure you're getting the most out of every endorsement you do get. In 2004, that's where the Entertainment Working Group came in.

Led by Mark Wallace, the deputy campaign manager, the group was assigned to recruit and find celebrities, entertainers, and athletes to attend and perform or speak at campaign events. Fairly early in the campaign, Mark invited me to join them. I agreed because I thought it might be interesting. I had no idea.

About once a week the group would get together to hear an update from Frank Breeden, director of entertainment for the Republican National Convention and former president of the Gospel Music Association. In some areas, such as country music, the president had quite a few supporters—performers like Brooks and Dunn, Sara Evans, and Darryl Worley. In other areas, such as pop music or movies, however, there weren't a lot of names to choose from, so whenever we talked about actors or pop musicians, the meeting quickly devolved into a game I called, "Which Celebrity Hates Us the Most?" We would sit around the conference room table and trade stories about what various celebrities had said about the race, the president, and my dad. One of my favorites was a statement by the actress Jessica Lange, who was so dedicated to defeating George W. Bush and Dick Cheney that she stood onstage at a Democratic fundraiser and in a moment of particularly high passion swore, "I'll do everything that I can possibly do, short of selling my children," an exemption I'm sure her children greatly appreciated.

Because the Bush-Cheney campaign's roster of celebrity endorsements was rather limited, the Entertainment Working Group focused most of its efforts on lining up talent for the Republican National Convention in New York City. It was the biggest event of the campaign and one that we, like the Democrats, had to work very hard to make entertaining.

Once upon a time, political conventions had built-in drama. The nominees were rarely a foregone conclusion and party leaders made back-room deals and swapped votes. It frequently took several ballots and much arm twisting before a candidate could secure the nomination. Stephen Douglas won on the fifty-ninth ballot in 1860, Woodrow Wilson on the forty-sixth ballot in 1912, and in 1924, it took John W. Davis 103 ballots to win the Democratic Party's nomination. But due to changes in election laws and in the rules regarding how delegates are chosen, today's nominees are usually known months before the conventions take place.

With much of the suspense gone, broadcast television networks have drastically cut back on the amount of air time they are willing to commit to convention coverage. In 1976, the networks dedicated one hundred hours to the national party conventions. By 2000, the figure had dropped to twenty-three hours. So every four years, the parties try to put on a show at their conventions, ever hopeful that the networks will pay more attention—or at least not pay less. The parties try to create spectacles, but organizers have to be careful because wherever there is a spectacle, a disaster may not be far behind.

At the 1948 Democratic convention, organizers wanted to do something dramatic to help raise the spirits of the delegates. Most polls showed Thomas Dewey, the Republican presidential nominee, holding a substantial lead over President Harry Truman, so as a morale booster, plans were made to release doves into the convention hall on the night of President Truman's acceptance speech. Unfortunately, by the time the doves were released from their cages high up in the rafters, most of them had died from heat exhaustion, and the surviving birds, disoriented, confused, and probably quite thirsty, proceeded to dive bomb the delegates.

The 2004 equivalent of dead doves were the balloons that wouldn't drop. Democratic convention organizers had arranged for more than a hundred thousand balloons and tons of confetti to rain down on the stage and the delegates at the conclusion of John Kerry's acceptance speech. When the speech ended, the music started playing, the delegates all stood up and cheered—and a few balloons floated down from the rafters, but nothing like the promised blizzard of balloons and confetti. Don Mischer, the convention producer, started yelling frantically into his radio, "Go balloons! Go balloons!" and for good measure, he even threw in a profanity or two. Like every other network, CNN was monitoring the radio for various programming cues, but unlike the other networks, CNN happened to broadcast the radio traffic live, so its audience got to hear Mr. Mischer's meltdown.

For the sake of drama, we thought about holding one night of the 2004 Republican National Convention at Yankee Stadium. The theme of the evening would be "America's Security in a Changing World," featuring someone like Rudy Giuliani as the keynote speaker, and it would conclude with a performance by a big-name musical group out in center field. We tossed around several ideas for who that music group should be. One suggestion was Aerosmith, even though it was kind of tough to imagine the group really fitting in with the evening. Try as I might, I just couldn't picture the delegates singing along to an Aerosmith song like "Love in an Elevator." Unfortunately, or possibly fortunately, due to scheduling conflicts and other logistics issues, the night at Yankee Stadium had to be pulled from the schedule.

Other proposed events that were designed to increase network appeal and coverage included a surprise visit to the convention by the president on Monday or Tuesday night, a big outdoor concert in Central Park or Battery Park, or possibly even having Dad give his acceptance speech via satellite feed from a symbolic venue like Ellis Island. Everyone liked the idea of Ellis Island, but it wasn't really feasible for Dad's acceptance speech. Since there was no big indoor space on the island, it would have to be an outdoor event, always risky due to weather and protesters. There wasn't enough space to accommodate all of the delegates and alternates, much less invited guests and VIPs. The media were spending millions of dollars on operations in Madison Square Garden and probably wouldn't have been real happy if we'd moved one of the biggest speeches of the convention to another site. And, most important, the plans for transporting people out to Ellis Island looked only slightly less complicated than the plans for the D-Day invasion of Normandy. Everyone would have had to go by ferry, we would have had to coordinate departure times from different piers up and down the length of Manhattan, and for security reasons, people would have had to wait on Ellis Island for several hours before Dad's speech. It was incredibly risky, too risky, and the idea was discarded fairly early in the planning process.

Even though the Ellis Island idea didn't work for Dad's acceptance speech, I still loved the idea of using it as the backdrop for an event. Ellis Island symbolizes the hopes and dreams of all the people who come to America to build new lives. The museum itself is historic and beautiful, and the island offers a spectacular view of lower Manhattan.

Kara Ahern, the deputy director of VP Operations, and I had spent weeks planning a rally to welcome my dad to the Republican National Convention, and Ellis Island seemed like the perfect location. We talked to the National Park Service to figure out where the stage and camera platforms should be set up. We rented the ferries that would be used to bring people in for the rally. We found a marching band to supply music for the event. We even had a backup plan in case of rain. Every contingency had been planned for, except one. We hadn't planned on the Kerry campaign trying to steal our camera shot.

A few days before the rally, I was with my parents on a campaign swing through Iowa, when my cell phone rang. It was Kara calling from Ellis Island. She had taken the advance team out there that morning for a walk-through of the rally site, when she heard a rumor from some of the Park Service personnel that John Kerry was going to visit the island that day for a surprise photo op. If Senator Kerry were to hold his photo op just a few days before our rally, it would look as if we were copying him, or at least, it would make our event seem unoriginal. We wanted to keep the Kerry campaign from using our site, but in a way that wouldn't end up in a confrontation or, God forbid, in the newspaper. Our only hope, we decided, was to make the site so unattractive that the Kerry campaign wouldn't want to use it.

We brainstormed and came up with a bunch of different ideas, everything from praying for rain to having several dozen volunteers in Bush-Cheney T-shirts and hats pose as a tour group and swarm the Kerry photo op, but Kara had the best idea of all—seagulls. Two staffers were quickly dispatched to the Ellis Island snack bar to buy as many french fries as they could carry, while the rest of the advance team spread out over the area they thought the Kerry campaign would want to use.

For the next four hours, Kara and the advance team stood in the hot sun, feeding french fries to most of the seagulls in the tristate area, while groups of tourists looked on in amazement and even snapped a few pictures. The team worked the birds into a veritable feeding frenzy, so that when Senator Kerry's advance team finally showed up, they were greeted by hundreds and hundreds of big, aggressive, noisy, defecating seagulls. The Kerry staffers took one look at the situation and decided to relocate their photo op. Our shot, and our rally, were saved.

Fortunately, the seagull episode was one of the few unplanned events of the convention. Organizers had spent over two years preparing for the Republican National Convention, and the program was planned down to thirty-second intervals. The broadcast networks were covering only three prime-time hours of the convention—one hour each on Monday, Wednesday, and Thursday nights—so it was absolutely critical that the program stay on schedule so that the key speeches and the key messages would be televised. Figuring out who would speak during those three prime-time hours, and for how long, was one of the toughest planning challenges.

A few of the speakers were given: President Bush would speak on Thursday, Mrs. Bush would speak on Tuesday, and Mom and Dad would speak on Wednesday, but after that it became a matter of balancing egos, message, and time. One governor would agree to appear only if he got one of the keynote slots and at least fifteen minutes of prime time. Requests from potential 2008 presidential candidates had to be balanced against each other so that no one could be accused of trying to anoint the next nominee. And everyone wanted to introduce the president.

One of the greatest fears of every convention planner is having the program run late because it means that the last speech of the night—usually the most important of the night—will be pushed out of prime time and risk being cut off by the networks. To help prevent this, all speeches are submitted for approval, both for content and for time. And as an added insurance policy, several short musical interludes are usually scheduled in each night's program as well. That way, if any of the speakers run over their allotted time, the convention organizers can simply pull the musical interlude and get the program back on schedule.

There are some speakers, however, that convention organizers cannot control no matter how hard they try. In 1988, at the Democratic National Convention in Atlanta, a little-known governor named Bill Clinton had been allotted fifteen minutes for his speech nominating Michael Dukakis. When the governor ran over time and showed no signs of stopping, the convention staff flashed the message "Governor, your time is up" on the teleprompter. But Bill Clinton went on for another seventeen minutes. Even the hardcore Democratic supporters at the convention were annoyed. They cheered the loudest when Governor Clinton said, "In conclusion." Given that no one wanted to be accused of giving the Republican version of Bill Clinton's 1988 nominating speech, most speakers did their best to stay on time.

The difference between a national convention that is nominating a challenger and one that is renominating a sitting president is enormous. Many of the decisions regarding the 2000 convention, including the decision to hold the convention in Philadelphia, had to be made long before George W. Bush was assured of winning the nomination. But every major decision regarding the 2004 convention was made in consultation with the Bush-Cheney campaign. In 2000, the key message coming out of the convention was a call for change. In 2004, it was about the need to stay the course, about portraying George W. Bush as a strong, decisive, and steadfast wartime president, and about showing how John Kerry lacked the qualities necessary to effectively lead the country.

For me, the big difference between the 2000 and 2004 conventions was that in 2000, it felt as if our family was embarking on a great adventure. Everything was new and exciting. By the time we arrived at the 2004 convention, I was already ready for it to be over. This was partly due to the fact that I'd been working on convention planning for over a year, and was looking forward to no longer having to worry about line-by-line program schedules, which performer was going to go on after Dad's speech, or seating charts for the vice presidential box. But I also wanted to get out of the media fishbowl that is a national political convention so I could go back to my job on the campaign.

I'd experienced a slightly scaled-down version of the fishbowl during the 2000 convention in Philadelphia. There were news stories and editorials about my sexual orientation, and so many captions on newspaper pictures identified me as "the lesbian daughter of" that I started to wonder if my name had been changed and no one had bothered to tell me.

In 2004, the media focus started several days before the convention, as my parents held a small town hall with about 150 people in Davenport, Iowa. A woman in the audience asked Dad about his position regarding same-sex marriage, and Dad said, "Freedom means freedom for everyone," and that marriage is an issue best left to the states to decide, but that President Bush sets the policy for this administration. He also happened to mention that he and Mom have a gay daughter.

I didn't hear the question or Dad's answer because I was standing out in the hallway talking to Kara on my cell phone about the seagull situation on Ellis Island, so the first I heard about it was during the motorcade ride back to the airport. Because Dad's position on gay marriage had been consistent all along and since it wasn't really news to anyone that I'm gay, I figured his comments might get a blurb or two in the paper, but that they'd probably get drowned out by all the stories leading up to the convention. I was wrong.

A few right-wing political groups put out statements saying how disappointed they were that Dad hadn't given his full support to the Federal Marriage Amendment. Gay political groups used Dad's response in ads targeting the president featuring the tag line, "What if it was your child, Mr. President?" And various political pundits argued about whether Dad's comments were part of a larger campaign strategy to reach out to more moderate voters (it was actually just Dad being Dad).

One of the strangest responses to Dad's comments, however, came from a reporter. For several weeks, this reporter had been working on a profile piece that would run during the convention. She'd done interviews with both of my parents, and had even traveled out to Jackson, Wyoming, to fly-fish with my dad. The only thing left to do was to get some B-roll footage of the reporter walking with my parents, and it was decided that the easiest thing to do was to shoot it at the welcome rally on Ellis Island.

The day of the rally was incredibly hot and humid, so Mom and Dad went into a tent to get out of the sun while the camera crew set up. The agreement had been that it would just be video, no questions, but right before they began filming, the reporter announced that she needed to ask about Dad's comments in Davenport. Everyone said no way. Dad had already addressed the issue, and while the campaign had agreed to shoot the video, no one had agreed to give an exclusive interview on the subject of same-sex marriage. The reporter insisted, so the traveling press secretary told her that if she didn't drop it, the whole thing would be off.

Most reporters probably would have given up at this point, but not this one. Instead, she ran past the press secretary and the Secret Service, into the tent where Mom and Dad were waiting, at which point she burst into tears, sobbing that her producer was insisting she follow up on Davenport and that it just wasn't fair that she didn't have a chance to do so. Confronted by a crying network reporter, Dad gave in—sort of. He waited patiently while the cameraman got into position, let the reporter ask about his comments, then looked right at her and said, "I've answered that question." That was the end of the interview, probably one of the shortest interviews in political history.

Even before the debate over the Federal Marriage Amendment, Heather and I had decided that we were going to be pretty low-key at the convention. We were there to support my dad, and I was there because I had a job to do. Neither of us wanted to make public appearances, give interviews, or speak from the podium. We talked about the possibility of going up onstage either after my dad's speech or after the president spoke. I was happier and more comfortable staying behind the scenes and getting my job done, and Heather, even more averse to stares and cameras than I am, said there was no circumstance under which she wanted to go onstage. "President Bush could officiate at a gay wedding, and I still wouldn't want to go up there," is how she put it. Even when Heather decides to dig her heels in, she always keeps her perspective and her sense of humor—it's one of the things I love about her. Since we knew that whatever we did, it was sure to end up being a news story, we decided to do what we wanted to do—stay off the stage.

While our decision would have been noticed under any circumstances, it was given extra attention due to a comment made by U.S. Senate candidate Alan Keyes two days before Dad's acceptance speech. During an interview with a satellite radio station, Mr. Keyes said, "The essence of family life remains procreation. If we embrace homosexuality as a proper basis for marriage, we are saying that it's possible to have a marriage state that in principle excludes procreation and is based simply on the premise of selfish hedonism." The interviewer then asked if that meant that Mary Cheney was a "selfish hedonist." Keyes replied, "That goes by definition. Of course she is."

I was actually more baffled by Keyes's comment than I was offended by it. I'd never met Alan Keyes and didn't understand why he felt it necessary to call me a selfish hedonist, but in all honesty, it wasn't something I was going to worry about. Keyes has always been seen as a fringe player in Republican politics. He came in as an emergency substitute after Jack Ryan was forced to drop out of the Illinois Senate race, and he was expected to lose to Barack Obama in the general election by at least thirty points (he ended up losing by 43 percent). When the campaign press office called to tell me about Keyes's comment and to let me know that reporters were asking if I wanted to respond, I said, "Why would I say anything? Everyone already knows it was a completely bizarre and inappropriate comment for him to make. It doesn't deserve a response."

Several months later, Alan Keyes's daughter came out publicly as a lesbian, and I couldn't help but wonder if his statement about me wasn't a reaction to his own daughter's sexual orientation.

Alan Keyes was hardly the first person to put an outlandish label on me. People on the far right have paraded around with signs calling me the Bride of Satan, and people on the far left have denounced me on the internet as a Nazi sellout. In general, I try to ignore most of the insults hurled from the political fringes, although I do sometimes find humor in the more outrageous comments. By and large my attitude is that if someone approves of me, great. If they don't, I'm sorry they feel that way—they're certainly entitled to their opinion, but I'm not going to lose a whole lot of sleep over it.

After Keyes's statement, speculation increased in the media and on the Internet about whether Heather and I would go onstage at the end of Dad's speech. We'd already decided that we didn't want to, and didn't really see a need to change our plans just because of Alan Keyes. We would go to Madison Square Garden and watch Mom and Dad speak, but then we'd wait to congratulate them until we saw them backstage.

Dad began his speech by talking about his grandfather, who, when my dad was born, suggested to his parents that they send a birth announcement to President Franklin Delano Roosevelt, who shared Dad's birthday, January 30. My dad pointed out that his grandfather had not gone to high school. For many years he had worked as a cook on the Union Pacific Railroad and lived with Dad's grandmother in a railroad car. But his modest circumstances hadn't stopped him from thinking that President Roosevelt should know of my father's arrival. "My grandfather believed deeply in the promise of America," Dad said, "and he had the highest hopes for his family. And I don't think it would surprise him all that much that a grandchild of his stands before you tonight as vice president of the United States."

It was a great way to talk about the dreams Americans have always had for upcoming generations and to lead in to the heart of his speech, which was about protecting our country and its future. As he laid it out, we stood at a defining moment. We had put in place policies and created new institutions to defend America, stop terrorist violence, and increase stability in the Middle East, and President Bush was committed to continuing those policies. As for John Kerry, well, he was for fighting "a more sensitive war on terror," my dad observed, "as though al Qaeda will be impressed with our softer side."

By the end of the speech, the audience was on its feet, shouting, "Four more years! Four more years!" Heather and I ducked out of the hall just as he was ending and headed down to my parents' hold room under the stage. After watching my dad sign the papers that officially named him the Republican nominee for vice president, we headed out to a party with friends. When I got back to the hotel, I made sure that everything was set for Mom and Dad's campaign trip to the West Coast, and counted the days to the next major event—only thirty-three days until the vice presidential debate.

CHAPTER 15

The Running Mate

John Kerry should have picked Dick Gephardt to be his running mate. The former congressman has a great personal story: His father was a teamster and drove a milk truck, and his mom was a legal secretary. He served fourteen terms in the House of Representatives, including four terms as the Democratic leader, giving him a level of experience that qualified him to be president. He is from Missouri, a key swing state, and has strong ties to organized labor, a key Democratic constituency. If John Kerry had made Dick Gephardt his running mate and sent him to critical areas such as eastern Missouri, western Pennsylvania, and Democratic strongholds in Ohio like Cleveland, he could have been a very effective messenger for the Kerry-Gephardt ticket.

John Edwards, the son of a textile mill worker from Robbins, North Carolina, is also from a working-class background, but rather than having spent decades in public service, like Congressman Gephardt, Edwards is a former personal injury lawyer who in 1998 managed to win a seat in the United States Senate by spending more than six million dollars out of his own pocket. On the campaign trail, John Edwards would use stories from his youth to try to gloss over the fact that he had become very wealthy as a trial lawyer, but all the colorful anecdotes couldn't hide his undistinguished Senate record. During his single term in the U.S. Senate, John Edwards was lead sponsor on a total of seventy-four bills, none of which made it to the floor for a vote, and as his term advanced, he missed so many votes and made so few visits to his constituents that his hometown newspaper referred to him as "Senator Gone." His biggest financial supporters were other trial lawyers, an important constituency for Democrats, but given President Bush's repeated calls for tort reform, not one that any Democrat had to worry about losing. And while Edwards did manage to come in second in the 2004 Democratic presidential primaries, the only state he actually won was South Carolina, a state the Democrats had absolutely no hope of winning in the general election.

Media coverage of John Edwards often focused on his looks and his hair—and the candidate seemed pretty aware of them himself. One popular video on the internet in 2004 captured him prepping his hair for a television interview. He starts off arranging his hair with his fingers while looking in the mirror of a small compact. Then, a technician comes into the frame, hands the senator an enormous comb, and holds the compact so he can get a better view of himself. After several moments of very precise and vigorous hair combing, the senator closes his eyes and waits patiently while the technician applies the hairspray. Finally, both John Edwards and the technician use their fingers and hands until every strand is smoothed into place. All in all, an impressive feat of hair care.

In all fairness, it is apparent that Senator Edwards didn't know the camera was rolling, and I'm sure he never intended for the American public to see the hair preparation, but it is still an amazing thing to watch. Maybe it's because I've spent so much time around my dad, who is admittedly follically challenged, but I had a tough time imagining any serious candidate for national office spending that much time worrying about his hair.

I was so convinced that John Kerry wouldn't pick John Edwards as his running mate that I bet five dollars on it with another campaign senior staffer. When I went to settle my debt, I asked him what had made him so sure it would be Edwards. "Easy," he said. "John Kerry will always take the political path of least resistance." He pointed out that Edwards had come in second in the race for the nomination and had been campaigning like crazy on behalf of Kerry, and for the VP slot, ever since. "Of course he was going to pick Edwards."

While I was disappointed at losing the bet, I was looking forward to watching Dad take on John Edwards in the vice presidential debate. Senator Edwards might have been a successful trial lawyer who was skilled at theatrics and stagecraft, but I was sure he wasn't up to going head-to-head with my dad in a substantive debate about domestic policy and foreign affairs. John Edwards was going to be completely out of his league.

Dad's debate prep in 2004 was very different from the prep in 2000. For one thing, he didn't have to get up to speed on the issues. He had been helping to govern the country for almost four years, and he had the policies and the issues down cold. He also would be debating someone who was very different from Joe Lieberman, the intelligent and thoughtful two-term senator from Connecticut, who had been Al Gore's running mate.

Before the vice presidential debate in 2000, my dad had studied Joe Lieberman's debating style and seen someone who was very good at using humor to attack his opponent. He watched tapes of Joe Lieberman's debates from his 1988 Senate race when he destroyed the incumbent, Senator Lowell Weicker, and Dad fully expected Senator Lieberman to be just as tough in the vice presidential debate, though in the end the senator did not go on the attack and neither did my dad. The two of them had a civil and substantive exchange that is still widely regarded as one of the best political debates in recent history.

The 2004 debates seemed unlikely to turn out that way. We were pretty sure that Senator Edwards would treat the debate like a trial and would use his time to try to prosecute President Bush and my dad, particularly on their handling of the war in Iraq.

Liz was in charge of Dad's debate prep operation in 2004, just as she had been in 2000, but there were some new faces on the debate team she oversaw. Dad asked Mary Matalin to attend the practice sessions this time around, so he could get the benefit of her input and experience, and he invited Steve Schmidt, director of rapid response for the campaign, to join as well. Steve knew more about John Kerry's and John Edwards's records than just about anyone else and was brilliant when it came to framing an argument or crafting a sound bite. Other people, such as Ken Mehlman and Matthew Dowd, the chief strategist for the campaign, attended whenever they could. The other new member of the debate team was also the newest member of our family. Liz had given birth to her fourth child, Philip, on July 2, 2004, and figuring that there's no such thing as being too young to get started in politics, she brought him to every practice session.

There were also a few very important holdovers from 2000, including Scooter Libby, who had been an advisor to Dad during that campaign and was now his chief of staff at the White House. Stuart Stevens and my brother-in-law, Phil, who had taken turns playing moderator Bernie Shaw in 2000, came back to play Gwen Ifill in 2004. And once again, Congressman Rob Portman was recruited to play the part of Dad's opponent. He watched all of the Democratic primary debates as well as videos of Senator Edwards's television appearances, and he had John Edwards down pat. He could imitate his speaking style, hand gestures, and even the way he used his fingers to brush his hair off his forehead.

The prep sessions were much less formal than they'd been in 2000. We still timed every answer to make sure it was within limits, and Rob Portman always stayed in character, but, since the goal of the sessions was to give Dad the opportunity to think about his answers, we would periodically stop and talk about a particular answer, or how we thought Senator Edwards might respond.

Fortunately, Dad didn't have to adjust to a new debate format, even though Senator Edwards sure wanted him to. Former secretary of state James Baker, who headed up debate negotiations for our side, and his counterpart, Vernon Jordan, pretty quickly came to an agreement on the formats for the three presidential debates, but the format for the vice presidential debate proved to be a sticking point. The Presidential Commission on Debates recommended, and Dad accepted, a *Meet the Press*–style format where Dad and Senator Edwards would be seated at a table with the moderator. The only problem was that John Edwards didn't want to accept any format where he would have to sit down. We all assumed that was because being seated would severely limit his ability to wander around the stage and use courtroom theatrics. He finally agreed to the Presidential Commission's recommendations, but only after it became obvious that his only other choice was to forgo the debate entirely.

Dad spent the day before the debate fly-fishing in Jackson with Rob Portman, and then our family had a nice, quiet dinner at home, free from discussion of debate strategy or tactics. Dad was ready. He didn't need any last-minute cramming or advice, and a day on the river ensured that he was relaxed.

The stakes for the vice presidential debate couldn't have been higher. Coming out of the Republican National Convention, most polls showed President Bush holding on to a comfortable lead, but now, a month later, the race had tightened, and the Kerry campaign seemed to have captured the momentum. The first presidential debate had been held on September 30 in Miami, and many political pundits had ruled it a victory for Senator Kerry, describing the president's performance as stiff and defensive. When one senior Bush staffer was asked what Dad's goal for the vice presidential debate should be, he memorably replied, "Make sure the gangrene doesn't get above the knee." It wasn't a particularly comforting thing to hear.

Six days later, we were at Case Western Reserve University in Cleveland, Ohio, for the final walk-through before the debate. The facilities at Case Western were great. Dad's hold room was well lit and comfortable. The auditorium was small but adequate. And the staff and media work areas were easily accessible. The only problem was that in order to get from his hold room to the stage, Dad had to walk through a hallway that was technically in John Edwards's area. According to the debate agreement, the candidates and their staffs weren't supposed to go into each other's area, but there really wasn't another option, so the Edwards advance team offered to grant us an exception.

I didn't want Dad to be rushed on his way up to the auditorium, so I walked the route with a couple of members of the advance team that afternoon to see how long it would take. Going through the door that connected our area to the Kerry-Edwards area was like walking into another world. Their side, like ours, was populated with lots of young staffers running around making final preparations, but on our side, they were going about their jobs in an upbeat but businesslike way. The rooms were neat, with two large Bush-Cheney '04 banners hanging on the walls. The Edwards team had wallpapered their area with hundreds of Kerry-Edwards signs, and as I looked into some of the rooms, I couldn't help but notice staffers lounging around on couches and used pizza boxes stacked up in the corner of one room. It felt like walking through a college dormitory on a Saturday afternoon.

The advance team was worried that walking Dad through a hallway plastered with Kerry-Edwards signs might throw him off right before the debate, so they suggested bringing in volunteers to line the hallway and wave Bush-Cheney signs to help get him pumped up. I understood and appreciated their concern, but knew it wasn't necessary. Dad didn't need to get pumped up. He was ready for this debate, and it was going to take a lot more than a bunch of Kerry-Edwards signs to throw him off his game.

To help cut down on distractions, we once again kept the number of people in Dad's hold room to an absolute minimum. Mom was the only person who was with him the whole time, and Heather, Liz, Phil, and I all went in to wish him luck before heading up to our seats in the auditorium. As she'd done in 2000, Liz gave Dad a small card to take onstage with him, but this time, the only thing written on the card was "Your children and grandchildren will never forget—and will tell their children and grandchildren—everything you have done for this great nation. We love you more than anything. Now go kick some butt."

When we got to our seats, Liz and I were a little surprised to see Senator Patrick Leahy sitting just a few feet away from us on the Edwards side of the aisle. Because the auditorium was so small, neither campaign received many tickets, and we used most of our allotment to take care of friends and family, people like Janet Rogers, who had been my mom's college roommate and served as maid of honor at my parents' wedding. When we saw that Senator Leahy was seated right in Dad's line of sight, we knew it wasn't a coincidence. We assumed it was an attempt by the Kerry-Edwards campaign to get under Dad's skin.

Some months before the debate, my father had had an exchange with Senator Leahy. In a press call with reporters, the senator had

made outrageous charges against my dad, accusing him of un-
ethical conduct regarding the awarding of Pentagon contracts to
Halliburton. The claims were untrue, and Senator Leahy had no
evidence to back them up, but that hadn't stopped him from making them. When he subsequently came up to my dad on the floor
of the Senate and tried to put his arm around him and act as
though they were the best of friends, my father, who has little
tolerance for hypocrisy, looked right at him, and said, "Go f——k
yourself," then turned and walked away. Dad didn't dwell on the
episode, and when questioned about it later during an interview,
he explained, "I expressed myself rather forcefully and felt better
after I had done it."

Apparently the Kerry-Edwards team was hoping that having
Patrick Leahy in the audience would somehow unsettle my Dad. It
didn't, of course, but Leahy's presence did signal a strategy that we
had suspected they might use. We had always thought that one of
John Edwards's goals for the debate would be to try to get my dad
to lose his temper. Patrick Leahy's presence in the audience told us
that we were right.

Gwen Ifill's first question was about Iraq. In his answer, Dad
laid out the reasons for going into Iraq and overthrowing Saddam
Hussein, and he concluded by saying, "We did exactly the right
thing." He didn't attack Senator Edwards's or Senator Kerry's positions on the war, although it would have been awfully easy to do.
Both of them were swinging away at the president out on the campaign trail even though they had both voted to authorize the use of
force in Iraq.

Senator Edwards chose to start his answer by saying, "Mr. Vice
President, you're still not being straight with the American people."
The tone of attack was one that he used throughout the debate as
he tried everything from accusing Dad and the president of mis-
leading the American people to accusing Dad of inappropriate be-

havior regarding the government's dealings with Halliburton, but Dad just kept his cool and kept coming back at him with facts, often about the senator's own record. I could tell that John Edwards was getting frustrated when Dad pointed out that he had missed thirty-three out of thirty-six meetings of the Judiciary Committee and 70 percent of the meetings of the Intelligence Committee. Senator Edwards's comeback was to charge that twenty years ago, while in Congress, Dad had voted against a ban on plastic handguns, an accusation so old and irrelevant that even the media didn't pursue it.

A little over halfway into the debate John Edwards took sleazy politics to a whole new level. Gwen Ifill asked a question about same-sex marriage, and Dad reiterated his belief that "freedom means freedom for everyone" and that individual states should be the ones to regulate marriage. Then it was John Edwards's turn. He said, "Let me say first that I think the vice president and his wife love their daughter." I was stunned. He *thinks* they love me? He's not sure, but he *thinks* they love me? What kind of thing was that to say? And then he did it again: "I think they love her very much." This was totally outrageous, particularly in the context of Ifill's question, because the implication was that since I'm gay, there might be some doubt about how they felt.

As Edwards went on to congratulate my family on the way they "embraced" me, I got angrier and angrier. What in the world gave John Edwards any right to comment on my family? What gave him the right to use my sexual orientation to try to score political points? Edwards was looking right at me, my mom, and Liz as he made these statements, and I was so furious that I didn't even think about it. I mouthed a phrase that, coincidentally enough, my dad had acquainted Patrick Leahy with just a few months earlier. My mom and Liz took a slightly higher road. Each of them separately made instantaneous mental calculations about what rude gesture they could send John Edwards's way that would not be noticed by the cameras or the audience behind us. And each of them, without consulting the other, stuck out her tongue at him. Edwards didn't miss a beat, but there was full-on eye contact, and he had to know that we thought he was complete and total slime.

Anyone watching my dad during the debate could see that he was just as mad as we were. He just did a better job of controlling his response. He knew that Edwards was trying to score political points by getting him to lose his temper and that the important thing was to stay calm and to close down the conversation. A vice presidential debate is never supposed to be about the candidates running for vice president, and it's certainly not supposed to be about their families. It's supposed to be about making the case for the candidate at the top of the ticket. If Dad had lost his temper and gone after John Edwards, it would have been the major news story of the debate, so Dad did something completely unexpected and very smart: He acted as though Edwards's smarmy comments had been sincere. When it was his turn to speak, he said, "Well, Gwen, let me simply thank the senator for the kind words he said about my family and our daughter. I appreciate that very much." Gwen Ifill looked at him and said, "That's it?" Dad replied, "That's it."

Looking back on John Edwards's comments, I have to admit that he handled the situation skillfully, just what I'd expect from someone who had won millions of dollars as a personal injury lawyer. He framed his statements in a way that was guaranteed to infuriate Dad and that would remind everyone in the known universe, particularly those who might object, that I was gay. Fortunately, Dad was too smart to fall for it.

Throughout the debate, Dad focused on defending the president's record and his handling of the War on Terror, he pointed out inconsistencies in Senator Kerry's record, and he even got in a few good digs at John Edwards's record, or lack thereof. One of the lines that got the most attention in the days following the debate was, "In my capacity as vice president, I am the president of the Senate, the presiding officer. I'm up in the Senate most Tuesdays when they're in session. The first time I ever met you was when you walked on the stage tonight." Dad honestly thought it was the truth. He had no recollection of meeting John Edwards at any time before the debate, and the senator said nothing during the debate to contradict that belief. But after the debate was over, Elizabeth Edwards made a beeline across the stage, heading straight for Dad. She went right up to him and said, "We did meet you! We did meet! At the prayer breakfast! We did meet!" Dad, still having absolutely no recollection of meeting the senator, but now destined to forever remember his wife, said, "That's nice," and turned to try to get away from the now very excited Mrs. Edwards.

As it turns out, Dad and John Edwards both attended the National Prayer Breakfast in 2001, and as photos taken at the breakfast showed, they were both seated at the head table. My mother remembered that Mrs. Edwards was there, because when Mom had made a joke about the difficulty of getting people to disagree with you once your husband assumes high office, Mrs. Edwards, apparently short on humor that day, had made a point of coming up to my mom and offering to disagree with her whenever she'd like. But Mom, like my dad, had no recollection of the senator. The Kerry-Edwards campaign tried to make a big deal out of the prayer breakfast, feeding it to the media and talking about it during interviews over the next few days, but if I'd been in their position, I probably would have released the photo and left it at that. As anyone who has met my dad knows, he's pretty good at names and faces. I've seen him walk down the street, bump into someone he met briefly twenty years ago, immediately recognize them, know their name, their family, and the subject of their last conversation. It's an impressive skill, and one I've seen him use hundreds of times over the years. If my dad doesn't remember meeting you, it means you made absolutely no impression on him whatsoever. If that was the case, I'm pretty sure I wouldn't want to brag about it.

Following tradition and protocol, when the debate was over, our whole family went onstage to congratulate Dad on having done such a great job, but, unlike in 2000, this time I had an additional special assignment. Everyone on the prep team had watched videotapes of John Edwards's speeches and previous debate performances, and we couldn't help but notice that there were a couple of characteristic gestures that he seemed to use at every event. The oddest was the half-mast thumbs-up he gave to the audience at the end of every speech. He would walk to the edge of the stage, stretch his arms out, place his thumbs on top of his fists, and then enthusiastically bend and unbend his arms a few times for emphasis. He'd usually finish the gesture off by brushing his hair off his forehead with his left hand.

Just before the debate, I was standing outside Dad's hold room talking to Liz and Scooter Libby. I'm not sure who exactly brought it up, but someone suggested that since I had the best imitation of the Edwards half-mast thumbs-up, it would be a good idea for me to do it onstage after the debate. Liz and Scooter thought this was such a great idea that they each offered to pay me one hundred dollars to do it, so after I congratulated Dad, I walked to the edge of the stage and did my best John Edwards impersonation. It was the sweetest two hundred dollars I ever earned.

Back at the hotel we had a victory party with a small group of close friends and family. Several TV sets were tuned to the post-debate coverage and analyses, and Joe Kildea, who ran the war room at the campaign, was sending me emails with quotes about the debate from all of the various political commentators. I would read the best ones out loud and everyone would cheer. Among my favorites were:

- Chris Matthews describing the debate between Dad and Senator Edwards as "The Howitzer" v. "The Water Pistol."
- Jim Geraghty of the *National Review* calling Dad's performance, "The single most devastating one-sided drubbing since Lloyd Bentsen smacked Dan Quayle all around the stage in 1988."
- Dick Morris saying, "Confronted with Dick Cheney's obvious competence, incisive parries to his charges, and devastating rebuttal of his phony statistics, Edwards looked like the proverbial deer in the headlights."
- John Podhoretz saying of Dad, "He banged on Edwards like a drum."

Even Don Imus, who was publicly supporting the Kerry-Edwards ticket, said Edwards "got killed" in the debate, but the best quote came from Mike Barnicle of the *Boston Herald*. He said the only thing about the debate that surprised him was "that at the end of the debate, at the end of the ninety minutes, Dick Cheney did not turn to John Edwards and say, 'By the way, give me the car keys, too.' "

It would have been a nice touch.

CHAPTER 16

Anybody but the
New York Times

When I can get my father to reminisce—which isn't often—he'll sometimes talk about the Ford campaign in 1976 and about some of the reporters who covered it. He speaks fondly of Aldo Beckman of the *Chicago Tribune,* and he talks about the great respect he has for Lou Cannon, who covered President Ford for the *Washington Post.* Tough but fair is how he'll describe these reporters. It was Cannon, he remembers, who made it clear that President Ford was in a whole lot of trouble after he said during the foreign policy debate with Jimmy Carter that "there is no Soviet domination of Eastern Europe and there never will be under a Ford administration." As my dad remembers it, he and Brent Scowcroft were briefing the press after the debate when Cannon shouted from the back of the room, "Hey, Cheney, how many Soviet divisions are there in Poland?"

Some of his best stories are about Jim Naughton of the *New York Times,* who was famous for his practical jokes. Naughton once sent telegrams to several of his colleagues informing them that they had been selected to ask questions at the next presidential debate. The excited reporters immediately called their offices to tell them the news, and then, when they found out that they'd been had, they had the humiliating task of calling back to inform their editors that, in fact, they would not be asking questions at the next debate.

Toward the end of President Ford's term, a few of Naughton's colleagues came up with a scheme to get him back for all of the jokes that he'd pulled on them over the years, and they recruited Dad to help them pull it off. Every news outlet was trying to secure an interview with President Ford to talk about his loss to Jimmy Carter and to get his perspective on his presidency. The reporters got Dad to call Naughton and tell him that he had an exclusive. "You're the guy, Jim," Dad told him. "The president wants to talk to you. You need to be up at Camp David Saturday morning at eight. Show up at the gate and they'll escort you up to Aspen lodge for the interview."

Since Dad was the White House chief of staff, Naughton fell for it hook, line, and sinker. He called the *Times,* told them to hold Sunday's front page, and arranged to have them fly in a photographer for the interview. To ensure that they would be on time for the early-morning interview, Naughton and the photographer drove up to Thurmont, Maryland, near Camp David, on Friday and spent the night at the Cozy Motel.

On Saturday morning, Dad was sitting in his office with the gang of pranksters, when the phone rang. It was the commandant up at Camp David reporting that two men were at the front gate claiming to have an interview scheduled with the president of the United States. The commandant was confused, because no one had told him about an interview, and the president wasn't even at Camp David. Dad asked the commandant to hand the phone to Jim Naughton. When Naughton picked up, he heard everyone laughing in Dad's office. He knew he'd been had, and he laughed right along with everyone else.

Two years later, Dad was lying in a hospital bed in Cheyenne, Wyoming, recovering from his first heart attack and trying to figure out how to keep his congressional campaign alive, when Mom brought him a telegram. It was from Jim Naughton and said, "Dear Dick. I didn't do it." At a time when there didn't seem to be a lot of humor in the universe, it gave my dad, and our whole family, a good laugh.

What strikes me about these stories is that reporters like Beckman, Cannon, and Naughton, who had prestigious beats and worked very hard at covering them, also understood that being an administration official, or, God forbid, a Republican, didn't necessarily make someone the enemy. I especially love the Naughton stories because they show a reporter who not only knew how to get in a good jab but could also take a joke. As far as I can tell, that doesn't happen very often anymore.

There is a series of annual dinners in Washington—the White House Correspondents dinner, the Gridiron Club, the Alfalfa Club, and the Radio and Television Correspondents dinner—that are all attended by lots of press people and that feature press stars and political celebrities as speakers. I've been to only one of these events, the Alfalfa Club dinner, but from everything I've heard and read, they all share the same goal: to skewer politicians. The press makes fun of politicians and the politicians make fun of politicians, but it is pretty rare for anybody, particularly any politician, to make fun of the press. At the height of the Monica Lewinsky scandal, President Clinton wowed the audience by referring to his legal troubles. "Please withhold subpoenas until all the jokes are told." President Bush has gotten enthusiastic receptions by making fun of his misadventures with the English language. One year, after he had declared in a speech that "we ought to make the pie higher," he told radio and television correspondents, "It is a very complicated economic point I was making there. Believe me, what this country needs is a taller pie." But even in the middle of the scandal about Jayson Blair, who made up and plagiarized stories that appeared in the *New York Times,* a joke about the *Times* nominating reporters for the Pulitzer Prize for fiction wouldn't have gone over well. One experienced speechwriter for events like the Gridiron Club warns politicians that if they poke fun at the press, they'd better be ready for stony silence from the crowd—or even boos and hisses.

The press takes itself pretty seriously these days, and having been through two national elections, I have to say that it looks as though some in the mainstream media have developed such exalted notions of themselves that they no longer consider informing the public to be their primary job. Instead, they feel a need to guide public opinion—away from George Bush and in the direction of whoever his Democratic opponent might be.

How else is it possible to explain what happened at CBS News with the story of the president's (supposed) National Guard papers? Just imagine for a minute that you are a producer for a network news magazine, and a controversial and persistent critic of the president provides you with documents supposedly written by a man now dead that are damaging to the president. Further imagine that you consult four document examiners, all of whom come to the conclusion that because the documents are copies, they cannot determine whether they are authentic. Two of the examiners are concerned that the typography does not look like typography from the time in which the documents were supposedly produced.

So, you have documents that can affect the election. They come from a doubtful source, cannot be authenticated, and even look suspicious. What do you do? You convince Dan Rather to run with them on *60 Minutes II,* and apparently, it's not a hard sell. Nobody seems particularly concerned, for example, that you haven't checked your source's story about where the documents came from. And, meanwhile, you contact the Kerry campaign so that they know the story is coming.

Everybody knows how this adventure turned out. Within hours of the airing of the piece on September 8, 2004, bloggers were pointing out some of the same problems that the document examiners consulted by CBS had noted—and more. A blogger named Buckhead pointed out that the memos, supposedly produced on typewriters, had proportional spacing rather than the monospacing that typewriters used in the early seventies. Power Line and Little Green Footballs weighed in as well. Little Green Footballs superimposed one of the *60 Minutes* memos over a document produced using Microsoft Word to show how close the two were. ABC News helpfully interviewed the two document examiners who had expressed reservations about typography to CBS.

CBS tried to stick to its guns, but ultimately CBS News president Andrew Heyward had to apologize for the segment. Then, in one of the oddest spectacles of modern journalism, Dan Rather began to claim that whatever the status of the documents, he still had faith in the underlying facts of the story. "Those who have criticized aspects of our story," he said, "have never criticized the heart of it, the major thrust of our report, that George Bush received preferential treatment to get into the National Guard, and, once accepted, failed to satisfy the requirements of his service." Rather's argument, which became famous as the "fake but true" defense, seemed to be a new kind of journalism, where what you believe (in this case about George W. Bush) trumps everything else, including the facts.

One of the striking things about the 2004 campaign is how open various members of the mainstream media were about where they stood. Early on in the campaign, there were more than a few dropped jaws at Bush-Cheney headquarters when we heard about a dinner that a handful of top staffers had with reporters and editorial writers at the *New York Times*. Nobody thought the *Times* would endorse the president or give him any kind of break, but we were taken aback when we heard that one of the *Times* staffers had declared at the end of the evening that they knew John Kerry wasn't perfect, that Kerry's positions, when he even had them, often didn't make sense, but that it didn't matter. The *Times* still wasn't going to support George W. Bush.

Early in the campaign, Evan Thomas of *Newsweek* appeared on the television show *Inside Washington* and said, "There's one other base here, the media. Let's talk a little about media bias here. The media, I think, wants Kerry to win and I think they're going to portray Kerry and Edwards, I'm talking about the establishment media, not Fox. They're going to portray Kerry and Edwards as being young and dynamic and optimistic and there's going to be this glow about them, collective glow, the two of them, that's going to be worth maybe fifteen points."

Less than a month before the election, ABC News political director Mark Halperin sent employees a memo telling them to quit worrying about old-fashioned notions of journalistic objectivity in their campaign coverage because the Bush team didn't deserve it. "Current Bush attacks on Kerry involve distortions and taking things out of context in a way that goes beyond what Kerry has done," he wrote, so there should be no more holding "both sides 'equally' accountable." To ABC's credit, at least one person there was sufficiently put off by the suggestion that the network ought to pound Bush harder than Kerry that he or she leaked the memo to Matt Drudge. It ran as an exclusive on his website, giving the world a chance to see how the political director of ABC News was coaching his team.

What sure looked like a double standard operating against the

Bush-Cheney campaign was sometimes demoralizing. I particularly found that to be the case when Ben Ginsberg, one of the best lawyers and nicest people I know, had to resign from his position as lead outside counsel for Bush-Cheney '04. The issue was the 527s, independent political advocacy groups that had sprung up in the wake of the Campaign Reform Act of 2002. From the beginning, it was clear that many of these supposedly independent groups had ties to Democrats. Jim Jordan, John Kerry's former campaign manager, served as a consultant for both America Coming Together and the Media Fund, and Bob Bauer, an attorney who was advising the Kerry campaign, was also advising America Coming Together. These connections were of little interest to the media, but on August 25, 2004, the *New York Times* ran a front-page article by Jim Rutenberg and Kate Zernike under the headline "Veterans' Group Had G.O.P. Lawyer." The article explained that Ben Ginsberg, lead outside counsel for the Bush-Cheney campaign, had given legal advice to the Swift Boat Veterans for Truth. The arrangement was perfectly legal, violated no campaign finance laws or regulations, and was nearly identical to the relationships that lawyers working for the Kerry campaign had with 527s like America Coming Together. But it was the Republican connection that got big play. Ben Ginsberg recognized the realities of the situation. It didn't matter that he had done nothing wrong. It didn't matter that a double standard was being applied. The media would continue to focus on him, making him a distraction for the Bush-Cheney campaign, so he resigned.

Perhaps the presence of Fox News and the growth of the blogosphere (where so far as I can tell, right-of-center bloggers play a more important role than left-of-center ones) help account for the increasingly open bias in some parts of the mainstream media. I know for sure that Fox News, the *Weekly Standard,* and blogs such as Powerline and Instapundit helped boost morale at the Bush-

Cheney campaign. They could be tough on President Bush and my dad, but at least they seemed to inhabit the same universe we did. The things they reported bore at least some resemblance to reality.

The communications staff of the Bush-Cheney campaign was completely realistic about the problem. One staff member explained to me that once you get used to the fact that the reporters will never be your friends, the daily interchange with a hostile press corps is actually pretty easy. You make sure they have the schedules, the hotel rooms, and the phone lines they need, which the Democrats, who take them for granted, often neglect to do. You treat them with total professionalism and just hope that from time to time they will respond in kind.

My dad had a somewhat different philosophy for dealing with hostile media: Don't waste time or resources on them. He knew the odds of getting a fair story out of the *New York Times,* in particular, were pretty much nonexistent, so why give them special access? The *Times* felt entitled to a seat on Dad's plane, but there were far more reporters who wanted to ride on *Air Force Two* (a privilege for which their organizations paid handsomely) than could be accommodated, so if choices had to be made, why choose the *New York Times?* Every now and then the communications staff would ask to have the *Times* included on a certain trip, and since I was both director of VP Operations and my father's daughter, I was usually the one nominated to bring it up with Dad.

In August 2004, we were on a campaign swing through Arkansas when I received several calls and emails from my sister, Liz; Nicolle Devenish, the campaign communications director; Anne Womack, the campaign press secretary assigned to Dad; and Mary Matalin, all telling me that a *Times* reporter was working on an in-depth profile of Dad and his relationship with the press, and that the reporter absolutely had to get on the plane. Dad immediately said no. I saw no reason to press the issue and emailed everyone to let them know that there was no room for the reporter on the plane. They all emailed me back and said the reporter had to get on the plane and that it was up to me to convince my dad to change his mind. I knew it was most likely going to be an impossible mission, but I was a team player and agreed to give it a try, so the next morning I went to his hotel room and told him how everyone—Mary Matalin, Nicolle, Liz, and Anne—thought it was vitally important that we take this reporter along. They were convinced that there was a chance that we would actually get a fair story out of this particular reporter, and they were worried that we would end up with an awful story if we didn't let him on the plane. Dad, who had been beat upon steadily by the *New York Times*, not just for months, but for four years, listened patiently, then looked at me over the top of his glasses and, in a completely calm voice, said, "Tell them it will be an even worse story when I kick the reporter out of the plane at thirty-five thousand feet." The *Times* reporter never did make it aboard.

In September, *New York Times* reporter Rick Lyman wrote one of the funniest stories of the campaign. Called "Desperately Seeking Dick Cheney," it was about his life on the road trying to cover Dad without ever setting foot on *Air Force Two*. He wrote:

> The Vice President travels on Air Force II. . . . A crew of about 10 reporters flies with him, representing all the networks, the wire services and two or three newspapers. There are snacks, cable television and camaraderie.
>
> But there is not a seat for me.

Lyman described two weeks in which he flew ten thousand miles commercially and traveled another thousand in rental cars. "My expense account will be a splendid thing," he wrote.

He described the small towns he visited, the food he ate, and the special status at least one of his colleagues granted him due to his pursuit of my dad. "A reporter from the Air Force Two pool sidled up to me," he wrote, "and said, 'I really admire what you're doing,' as though I was marching from Selma."

Lyman wrote about the people he encountered, a Kerry supporter in Minnesota who was irritated at not being able to get into one of my dad's town meetings and a teacher in New Mexico who liked my dad:

> "I found the Vice President to be very warm, very trustworthy," said Elaine Schoman, an English and Spanish teacher at Cuba High School in Cuba, NM, just after she was one of a dozen hand-picked supporters to have breakfast with the Vice President on Thursday. "Which publication did you say you were from?"
>
> An icy look passed quickly over her face. "You need to talk to your people," she said. "You're all twisted in one direction."

Lyman's article was so good-humored that my dad considered relenting and allowing him on the plane, but in the end, he didn't, and given how the New York Times behaved during the final days of the campaign, there's no doubt that it was the right decision.

On Monday, October 25, the Times ran a lengthy front-page article under the headline "Huge Cache of Explosives Vanished from Site in Iraq." The story was about 380 tons of explosives that had disappeared from the Al Qaqaa weapons storage facility in Iraq, and the Times bludgeoned us with the missing weapons cache through the rest of the campaign. They ran story after story, including three more on the front page. In eight days, there were sixteen stories and columns on Al Qaqaa and more than half a dozen letters to the editor. Then came the election, and the *New York Times*' concerns about Al Qaqaa seemed to magically disappear.

A search of the *Times*' own archives shows that in the four months after the 2004 election, there was exactly one mention of Al Qaqaa in the *New York Times*, in a story that was unrelated to the issue of the missing explosives. It wasn't until March 13, 2005, that there was any sort of follow-up, and that came only after the *National Review*'s Byron York wrote a piece titled, "Remember Al Qaqaa?" York asked, "Why was the Al Qaqaa story so important in the eight days leading up to the election that it merited two stories per day, and so unimportant after the election that it has not merited any stories at all?" York asked the public editor of the *New York Times*, Daniel Okrent, if it didn't look as though the *Times* was pushing the story only when it might influence the outcome of the election. "I would say at the very least," Okrent told York, "that the dates they were running stories certainly can leave an impression."

And it certainly did.

CHAPTER 17

A Cheap and Tawdry
Political Trick

John Kerry didn't "out" me, nor did he offend or attack me by calling me a lesbian. It wasn't a secret that I was gay, and I certainly couldn't be offended by the truth. What was offensive about his decision to bring me up in the third debate was that he was so obviously trying to use me and my sexual orientation for his own political gain. It was, as my mom so accurately described it, "a cheap and tawdry political trick."

I'd watched the first two presidential debates with my parents, but not the third. Dad was scheduled to do several postdebate television interviews, and I knew he wanted to concentrate on the debate, so I went down the hall and watched with a couple of other staffers while we worked on the travel schedule for the final two weeks of the campaign. Since we were working and talking, I was only halfway listening to the debate, but when Bob Schieffer asked, "Do you believe homosexuality is a choice?" it got my attention, partly because I was curious to see how the president and Senator

Kerry would answer, but primarily because it was such an unexpected question.

The third debate was supposed to focus on domestic policy, and I was pretty sure there would be at least one question about gay issues. Same-sex marriage had been a topic of debate throughout the campaign, so I assumed that the moderator would ask about gay marriage or about the Federal Marriage Amendment. But it never occurred to me, or anyone else in my family, that the moderator might ask if homosexuality was a choice.

From Senator Kerry's answer, I'd say he and his debate prep team hadn't anticipated the question either. They must have practiced for a question on gay issues, and I'm certain that they had decided that whenever the question about gay issues came up, Senator Kerry should work me into his answer, noting, perhaps, that the Cheney family, who knew about these things firsthand, didn't support a constitutional amendment.

But Bob Schieffer didn't ask about same-sex marriage or the Federal Marriage Amendment. Instead, he came at the subject from a completely unexpected angle, and John Kerry, a man with whom I've never so much as exchanged a single word, was suddenly talking to millions of Americans and claiming to know my personal thoughts and beliefs. He said, "We're all God's children, Bob, and I think if you were to talk to Dick Cheney's daughter, who is a lesbian, she would tell you that she's being who she was, she's being who she was born as."

Whenever they've been asked about it by the media, anyone who was associated with the Kerry campaign or with Senator Kerry's debate preparation has claimed that his reference to me was spontaneous and unplanned, that it was not part of some campaign strategy. I'd probably be a lot more willing to believe those claims if not for the fact that both Senator Kerry and Senator Edwards made a point of bringing me up in their answers to debate questions about gay issues. I suppose it could have been a coincidence. I guess it's possible that I am the only gay person that either of them has heard of, but given that there are millions of gay people in the United States, including well-known celebrities, political activists, and even a few Democrats, I find that difficult to believe.

I think that both John Edwards and John Kerry were prepped to include a reference to me and my sexual orientation in any answer they gave to a debate question regarding gay issues. The only difference between the two was that John Edwards got a question about same-sex marriage—a question he had prepared for. John Kerry didn't. Senator Kerry and his debate prep team didn't anticipate a question about whether sexual orientation is a choice, and by forcing "vice president's daughter" and "lesbian" into his response, he ended up giving an answer that struck most people as jarring and inappropriate. Aides to Senator Kerry even admitted to *Newsweek* that the reference was in poor taste. One top Kerry advisor called it "klutzy," which it certainly was, but it was also much much more.

I can't be sure why the Kerry campaign targeted me. I've heard lots of theories: that it was an attempt to drive a wedge between the Republican ticket and evangelical Christian voters; that the Democrats wanted to spotlight what they perceived to be the hypocrisy of a Republican candidate having an openly gay child; that it was an effort to shore up support for John Kerry among African-American voters, who tend to oppose extending legal protections to gays and lesbians by greater margins than their Caucasian counterparts.

Whatever the reason, I was furious. Everyone else in the room froze when Senator Kerry gave his answer, but I was not at a loss for words. I turned toward the TV and said, "You son of a bitch." It was a blatant and sleazy political ploy made even more obvious by his awkward answer. He had been bound and determined to work me into his answer no matter how weird it sounded. Moreover, he had used the word "lesbian," instead of the more common and politically neutral term "gay." He was going for maximum impact, and he got it.

I was so mad that I couldn't concentrate on finishing the travel schedule, so I went down to my parents' suite to watch the rest of the debate. Dad was sitting in front of the television, trying to focus on the end of the debate. He was angry, but he was also scheduled to speak at a postdebate rally and to do several interviews, so he had to make sure he heard everything that was said. My mom was so mad that she couldn't sit still, so she'd gone into the bedroom to keep from distracting Dad. Liz, who had been watching the debate with my parents, summed up the situation best when she declared John Kerry to be "a complete and total sleazeball."

As soon as the debate was over, Scooter Libby and Anne Womack, the campaign press secretary, came into the suite and we all got on the postdebate conference call with Steve Schmidt, the campaign's director of rapid response. The call had been scheduled well in advance so that Dad would have the same talking points that all of the campaign's surrogates were using in their interviews, but it quickly changed into a conversation about what a slimy thing John Kerry had done. Dad told Steve that he wanted to hit back and wanted to know if there was any reason why he shouldn't. Steve said, "Well, sir, as long as Mary's comfortable with it, I don't see any reason not to." I didn't even wait to be asked. I looked at my dad and said, "Make it hurt."

Mom wasn't scheduled to speak at the postdebate rally, but during the conference call she said that she really wanted to. She thought that what John Kerry had done was inexcusable and she wanted to call him on it. Steve asked her what she was going to say, and Mom replied, "That this is a man with a dark hole in his soul. He can have all the fake suntans and manicures he wants," she went on, referring to some of the spa stops Senator Kerry had made during the campaign, "but deep down inside, he's rotten." There was dead silence on the phone and shocked looks on the faces of the staffers in the room. I could tell they were thinking, "Oh my God—is she really going to say that?"

In the few minutes before the rally downstairs, we watched some of the postdebate coverage. I don't know what, if anything, could have stopped my mom from hitting back at John Kerry, but after we saw an interview with Mary Beth Cahill, Kerry's campaign manager, on Fox News, I knew I sure wasn't going to try to hold her back:

> **Chris Wallace:** Let me ask you about a point that Jim Angle just brought up and a number of us noticed. Is it over the line for John Kerry to bring up the fact that Dick Cheney's daughter is a lesbian?
>
> **Mary Beth Cahill:** Well, you know, I think that is an acknowledged fact. She seems to be very proud and open about her sexuality. Her parents seem to be very proud of her. And she has been a subject of the campaign off and on. I think Senator Kerry was just acknowledging . . .
>
> **Chris Wallace:** But she's not talking about it. Should he be talking about it?
>
> **Mary Beth Cahill:** Well, I mean, it comes up. There are a lot of questions here about gay marriage, and she is someone who's a major figure in the campaign. I think that it's fair game, and I think she's been treated very respectfully.

Fair game? My sexual orientation is *fair game?* It was completely outrageous. If President Bush had mentioned Dick Gephardt's gay daughter during the debate, and if Ken Mehlman, the Bush-Cheney campaign manager, had given an interview declaring her sexual orientation to be "fair game," the Kerry campaign, the Democratic Party, and every major gay and lesbian organization in the country would have been howling for blood. Any chance that we were going to hold back was gone. We were going to make absolutely certain that everyone in America knew exactly what our family thought of Senator John Kerry.

As our group of family, staff, and Secret Service agents determinedly marched downstairs, I couldn't help but notice that everyone, particularly Anne Womack, looked a little nervous. Nobody knew what Mom was going to say, but whatever it was, Anne was going to have to field all of the media calls.

In all the commotion and agitation, I'd forgotten to tell the advance staff or Sarah Straka, mom's personal aide, that Mom was going to speak. Normally, adding a speaker to the program is simple. It's just a matter of having the announcer add the person to the list, but that's not quite the case with Mom, because whenever she speaks from behind a podium, she needs Alta.

At five feet, maybe, Mom has trouble seeing the audience over the top of most podiums, so she always stands on something. Over the years, she has used phone books, briefcases, and even an old milk crate as stepstools during her speeches. During the 2000 campaign, Stephanie Lundberg, who first worked for my mom at the American Enterprise Institute and had volunteered to help her out during the campaign, asked her dad to build a step, basically a box, that Mom could travel with whenever she had to use a podium. In keeping with our family's WHCA call signs, which all start with the letter A, a couple of staffers named the box "Alta," Latin for high. In 2004, Alta went to every one of Mom's campaign events—every campaign event except the postdebate rally in Coraopolis, Pennsylvania.

It wasn't until Mom was getting ready to go onstage that any of us realized that we'd left Alta upstairs. Rather than wait for someone to go get it, Mom walked up to the podium, stood on her tiptoes, pulled the microphone down to her level, and let John Kerry have it with both barrels. "I did have a chance to assess John Kerry once more. And the only thing I could conclude is this is not a good man. This is not a good man. And, of course, I am speaking as a mom and a pretty indignant mom. This is not a good man— what a cheap and tawdry political trick." I thought it was great, even if she had dialed her rhetoric back quite a bit from what she'd said upstairs.

I knew that John Kerry's comment would result in some news stories, particularly after Mom announced to the world that he was "not a good man," but it wasn't until I watched the morning news shows the next day that I understood just how big a story it had become. Every morning show led with his reference to me, and the cable news channels had an all-day parade of experts on to discuss the story.

The Kerry campaign could have done a lot to defuse the situation simply by releasing an apology, but instead, they went into full crisis mode—defending Kerry's comment and coming up with all sorts of explanations to justify it. The most popular explanation coming out of the Kerry campaign was that he was trying to show respect for how strong families deal with this issue, a claim that stretched credibility to the limit since it didn't have anything to do with what he actually said, but even that wasn't as strange as some of the excuses various Democratic spokespeople came up with:

• Howard Wolfson, spokesman for the Democratic National Committee, said, "Dick Cheney has mentioned this on the campaign trail, so I'm not sure why it's OK for Dick Cheney to do it, but not John Kerry." I thought the answer was pretty obvious. It was OK for Dad to do it because he is my dad. As far as I'm concerned, John Kerry is more than welcome to talk all he wants to about his own daughters.

- Debra DeShong, a Kerry campaign spokesperson, said, "This is not a young girl who cannot defend herself, or talk about who she is and talk about her campaign and her family." While I certainly appreciate Ms. DeShong's faith in my abilities (if not necessarily her comment about my age), if Senator Kerry's comments weren't meant as an attack, why would I have to defend myself?
- John Edwards went on the MSNBC show *Hardball* and explained that John Kerry was just trying to put "a personal face on an issue that has been used to divide this country." I just thought it was kind of interesting that the face he chose to put on it happened to belong to the daughter of his opponent's running mate.

But the strangest response from the Kerry campaign came from Elizabeth Edwards. The day after the debate, she took part in an interview with ABC Radio. When she was asked about Senator Kerry's statement and about Mom's response, she said that Lynne Cheney "overreacted to this and treated it as if it's shameful to have this discussion. I think that's a very sad state of affairs—I think that indicates a certain degree of shame with respect to her daughter's sexual preferences—it makes me really sad that that's Lynne's response." I couldn't believe it. After having proclaimed how I must think and feel, the Kerry campaign was now psychoanalyzing my mom and our family in a totally insulting way. Admittedly, it's not that unusual for spouses to get attacked during campaigns, but usually it's done with at least a little more subtlety than this. As far as I can tell, it's the first time one candidate's wife has publicly attacked another candidate's wife by accusing her of being a bad mother.

Elizabeth Edwards's comments about my mom were in the same league as Alan Keyes's calling me a "selfish hedonist" during the Republican National Convention. They were so completely over the top that there was no sense in responding to them. Anybody who placed any credence in what either Edwards or Keyes had to say was so far gone that we were never going to reach them. The comments they made were so bizarre that they weren't even worthy of a response.

Not everyone agreed, however. Talk radio hosts and conservative bloggers on the Internet were thoroughly outraged by Elizabeth Edwards's attack on my mom. As Rush Limbaugh said on his radio show, "I'll tell you. This view, 'a certain bit of shame'? How in the world does she have the audacity to speak without knowing Lynne Cheney, without knowing this family, without being intimately aware of how this family lives?" The only thing Elizabeth Edwards accomplished was to pour more fuel onto the fire of what was already a hideously bad storyline for the Kerry campaign.

I couldn't help but notice how various gay and lesbian organizations reacted during this episode. Groups such as the Human Rights Campaign (HRC) and the National Gay and Lesbian Task Force (NGLTF) issued press releases stating that John Kerry's reference to me and my sexual orientation during the debate was appropriate, and several openly criticized Mom's reaction as being part of a phony political ploy, but as far as I can tell, none of them ever criticized Elizabeth Edwards for using the very politically incorrect phrase "sexual preferences." That phrase implied that she thought sexual orientation was a matter of choice, and contradicted the position that John Kerry laid out during the presidential debate. If Mom had used the term "sexual preference" during a speech or an interview, or God forbid, during her denunciation of John Kerry, I have no doubt that those same organizations would have attacked her for using "homophobic language."

In a campaign with many memorable and strange events, the period following the final presidential debate had to have been the most bizarre. I'd spent the past eighteen months working behind the scenes on the campaign and trying to maintain a low profile, but after the debate, I suddenly found my private life a topic of debate on the Sunday morning talk shows. When I saw an editorial in the *Wall Street Journal* titled "The Outing of Mary Cheney," I had to admit that I'd pretty much failed at the whole low-profile thing.

If the intent of the Kerry campaign had been to drive a wedge between the Republican ticket and evangelical Christians or to otherwise improve Kerry's standing in the polls, their strategy backfired spectacularly. Republican voters were fired up by the whole episode, while swing voters and even some Democratic voters saw it as a sleazy trick. Internal tracking polls in the days after the debate showed a noticeable improvement in the president's standing among likely voters in the battleground states. At the campaign, people referred to it as the "Mary Cheney bounce."

About a week after the debate, I was sitting in my office when a very junior staffer came in and asked me what it was like to be at the center of such a huge controversy, one that could possibly affect the outcome of the election. As she put it, "That's got to be so cool." I couldn't help but smile as I replied, "Yeah—it's an illustrious club, all right. Willie Horton, Gennifer Flowers, and me."

CHAPTER 18

Election Night 2004

Early numbers are always wrong. The exit polls were wrong in 2000, and they were going to be proven wrong in 2004. At least that was what I kept telling myself during the early afternoon of November 2, after I got the first round of exit poll results. They showed the president trailing in Florida, Ohio, and Iowa, states that we had to carry if we were going to win. The first numbers were so bad that I couldn't bear to pass them on to the rest of the staff. I knew that it wouldn't take long before they got them off the Internet or from members of the traveling press corps, but I didn't want anyone to start worrying any sooner than necessary. If the numbers were right, there wasn't anything that we could do to change the outcome, and I certainly didn't need to add to anybody's stress level. The staffers traveling back to Washington, D.C., on *Air Force Two* were already completely drained and exhausted. In the last two days of the campaign, we had traveled to Romulus, Michigan; Fort Dodge, Iowa; Los Lunas, New Mexico; Honolulu, Hawaii; Colorado Springs, Colorado; Henderson, Nevada; Sparks, Nevada; and Jackson, Wyoming.

The last-minute addition of a late-night rally in Honolulu had provided a wonderful boost for morale, but in order to fit it into the schedule we had to fly there and back in a single night. By the time we began our approach into Jackson, the last stop on a very long day, the aisles of the plane were clogged with exhausted staffers who had stretched out on the floor to sleep. We'd flown over ten thousand miles and had been campaigning for almost forty hours without a break.

The rally in Jackson revived us. It felt more like a homecoming or a class reunion than a political campaign event. Instead of giving their standard stump speeches, Mom and Dad told stories from past campaigns, including one about Dad's first trip to Jackson as a candidate for Congress back in January 1978, when he drove an old Ford all over the state meeting with voters and looking for support. Twenty-six years later he had come home to Jackson for his last rally as a candidate, only now he was campaigning for re-election as vice president of the United States and he was traveling on *Air Force Two*.

A few people at the campaign had argued that we shouldn't hold a rally in Jackson the night before the election. Everyone knew that we would win Wyoming by at least thirty points (we actually won it by almost forty), and they thought it made more sense to have Dad do an event in a battleground state. Maybe it did, but when I walked into the airport hangar and saw all of those friends waiting to welcome my parents home, I knew we'd made the right decision. Heather had flown into Jackson to meet us, and she agreed that it was the perfect way to end the campaign.

Early the next morning, after my parents voted at the local fire department, we headed for Waukesha, Wisconsin, where my dad was going to thank the volunteers at a Republican Party phone bank for all of their hard work. The volunteers gave my parents a warm reception, but their mood was noticeably subdued. It was pretty obvious that they'd heard about the exit polls.

I was still feeling pretty good about our chances as we took off from Waukesha en route to Washington, D.C. The exit polls were bad, but they'd been bad in 2000 and we still won. Mom and Liz were both cautiously optimistic, and Dad, as always, was confident that we were going to win. He'd taken one look at the exit poll results and said that something was wrong. There was no way that John Kerry had picked up that much support during the last weekend of the campaign. It wasn't until we were back at the Vice President's Residence getting ready for dinner that I really started to worry. I called the strategy department to get the latest update and was told, "If the numbers don't change, we could be in for a really long night," which is campaign-speak for "there's a really good chance that we're going to lose." Exit polls still showed John Kerry leading by almost 3 percent nationally, with higher-than-expected turnouts among women and African-Americans—two groups that tend to favor Democratic candidates by pretty significant margins. I felt sick to my stomach. I just didn't want to believe that we'd come this far and worked this hard only to lose. It took a few minutes and a pep talk from Heather, who reminded me how wrong the exit polls had been in 2000, before I was able to put on a brave face and go downstairs to watch the returns.

Most of the campaign staff, key donors, and friends and family were watching the returns downtown at the Ronald Reagan Building, but Mom and Dad had decided to spend the evening at the Vice President's Residence with a smaller group: Heather and me; Liz and Phil; Don and Joyce Rumsfeld; Al and Ann Simpson; Nick and Kitty Brady; Scooter Libby and his wife, Harriet Grant; and Mary Matalin. We all gathered around the bank of televisions set up in the living room and waited for the first results to come in.

Indiana and Kentucky, two dependably Republican states, closed their polls at 6:00 P.M. E.S.T. and were quickly called for President Bush, but when the next round of states closed their polls, at seven, the calls were much slower in coming. In 2000, the networks rushed to call Florida for Vice President Gore and then were forced to take back their call. None of them wanted to repeat that mistake, so they were all taking their time. We quickly noted that the actual vote totals being shown on television and on the Internet didn't match the results coming out of the exit polls. In some cases, they weren't even close. According to the exit polls, Virginia was supposed to be too close to call, but the vote counts coming in showed President Bush with a comfortable lead (he won the state by eight points). The exit polls also showed that Kerry had closed to within four or five points of the president in John Edwards's home state of North Carolina, but the vote count wasn't even close (President Bush would end up winning the state by fifteen points). A little after 8:30 P.M., I received an email from the strategy staff confirming what we'd all started to suspect—there were major problems with the exit polls, and over the next few hours it became increasingly apparent that we were going to win.

But the cautious networks wouldn't call the race, so the evening wore on. The living room grew colder as the hour grew later, but since my dad likes cool rooms and since this was his night, no one had the nerve to touch the thermostat. We hauled out blankets instead, and in some of the photos taken that evening, the women are huddled under a motley assortment of quilts and car robes. Liz, who had the world's worst cold and was hoping to isolate her virus, made herself a nest on the floor in a corner behind Don Rumsfeld and Al Simpson. Propped against a wall, she clicked away on her BlackBerry, passing along good news about Ohio that Mary Matalin was getting from Ken Mehlman. One of the people Liz was emailing was Margaret Tutweiler, who was having a party that included many journalists. Since we knew that some of them might go on air before polls closed in the West, we wanted to make sure that they had all the facts.

By 1:00 A.M., all the networks had President Bush within a single state of the 270 electoral votes needed for victory, and our family left for the White House. The plan was to meet the Bush family there, and then we would all go over to the victory party at the Reagan Building. I gave some thought to skipping the White House and going straight to the party at the Reagan Building with all of our friends and family and with the other staffers from the campaign, but I told myself it wouldn't be long before the networks declared President Bush and Dad the winners and Heather and I could go over with my family then. Apparently, I had learned absolutely nothing from election night in Austin four years earlier.

In the family quarters of the White House, the Bush family had gathered and everyone was in a great mood. My eldest niece, Kate, who was ten, had come with us, and President Bush forty-one immediately made her feel welcome. He said to her, "You know, you're the youngest person in the room and I'm the oldest. We ought to talk." The two of them sat on a large chair in the corner and had a conversation that went on for more than an hour.

We kept expecting to go over to the victory party any minute, but it became increasingly clear that no major news outlet was going to call the race until one of the candidates conceded—and John Kerry wasn't about to concede. The Kerry campaign was hanging tough. Even though it was obvious that President Bush had won Ohio, Mary Beth Cahill, Senator Kerry's campaign manager, went on television and declared that the state was going to put them over the top. Around two-thirty in the morning, John Edwards finally went onstage at Copley Square in Boston and told the waiting crowd, "John Kerry and I made a promise to the American people that this election, every vote would count and every vote would be counted. Tonight," he said, "we are keeping our word and we will fight for every vote. You deserve no less." There didn't seem to be any way for John Kerry to win the election, but they still weren't ready to give up.

Karl Rove had set up a mini war room in the old family dining room of the White House residence, where staffers were monitoring vote totals as they came in from each state. There weren't anywhere near enough outstanding provisional ballots to change the outcome in Ohio, and no one in the room had any doubt that President Bush and Dad had been re-elected, but nobody was quite sure what to do next. Just as in 2000, there was some talk about declaring victory even though the other side hadn't conceded, but the idea was quickly discarded. It would only inflame the Democrats and the Kerry campaign, and the media were sure to cast it in a negative light, so instead, Andy Card, the White House chief of staff, was dispatched to the Reagan Building to declare that, despite the delay, the Bush-Cheney campaign was certain of its victory.

Much of the crowd had been there since 8:00 or 9:00 P.M., so by the early hours of November 3, everyone was looking for places to sit down and take a break. I was getting emails from people who had the good luck to commandeer a sofa and weren't about to give it up. Carpeted sections of the floor were also highly valued, and at least one young staffer, so I was told, caught a nap by stretching out under one of the buffet tables.

All of the speakers and entertainers were in a holding room backstage, and periodically they were sent out to say a few words or sing a couple of songs to help keep the crowd energized. Ed Gillespie, chairman of the Republican National Committee, would stretch out and take a nap on one of the sofas in the hold room for twenty or thirty minutes, then wake up and go back onstage to say a few enthusiastic words before returning to his sofa. Country singer Darryl Worley and his band performed late into the night. It wasn't until after 2:00 A.M. that they finally called it a night. As they told the stage coordinator, "There's just no music left. We've played it all."

Once it was clear that nothing else was going to happen until morning, Dad suggested that Mom, Liz, Phil, Heather, and I all go home and get some sleep while he stayed at the White House. None of us wanted to risk missing out on the victory celebration, so we left the residence and found places in the West Wing where we could sleep for a few hours. Liz and her daughter, Kate, slept on sofas in the Roosevelt Room, as did Mary Matalin. Phil sat in Dad's outer office with David Bohrer, the White House photographer, and Jen Field, Dad's personal aide. Dad, Heather, and I were in his office. He was in his desk chair with his feet up on his desk, I was lying on the not very padded couch, and Heather was stretched out between a couple of armchairs. Mom was in the White House medical unit, not because she was ill, but because when she stepped off the elevators, she'd spotted the medical offices and thought they might have a bed. They did have one, a Murphy bed that pulled down from the wall. The staff on duty generously offered to make it up for her, but in the meantime, she lay down on one of the examining tables and fell asleep, and that's where she spent the rest of the night.

Just before sunrise, we all gathered in Dad's office and agreed that it would probably be best to go back to the Vice President's Residence and get some real sleep, or at least a shower. I tried to take a nap when we got back, but was too anxious and excited. I was sitting in the second-floor family room watching the cable news shows with my mom when Dad called to let us know that John Kerry had just phoned the president to concede the election. We were all supposed to meet at the White House that afternoon so we could ride to the Reagan Building for a delayed victory celebration. I was so happy that we'd won that I almost forgot about my clothing problem.

Having spent most of the last month on the road, I was officially out of clean clothes. When we got back to Washington, I'd sent my dirty suits to the cleaners, holding back one black one, the cleanest of the bunch, to wear on election night. But now I'd spent the night in it, and it looked much the worse for wear. Since I didn't have any other options, I steamed out as many of the wrinkles as I could in the shower (a trick I'd learned during the 2000 campaign) and just hoped that no one looked too closely.

In the rush to get ready, Heather and I hadn't had a chance to decide whether we would go onstage with the rest of the family for the president's speech, and it wasn't until we were in the hold room backstage at the Reagan Building that we even discussed it. I wanted to celebrate with my family, with all of our friends and relatives, and with all of my coworkers from the campaign. I wanted to go onstage, but I didn't want to go without Heather. She wasn't any more thrilled about going onstage at the Reagan Building than she'd been about going onstage at the Republican convention in New York—too many cameras—but she understood how important it was to me, so she smiled and walked out with me, a gesture I greatly appreciated.

Being on that stage was absolutely amazing. The floor was overflowing with cheering supporters and staffers. There were people packed four and five deep on the upper levels of the atrium leaning over the railings and yelling and screaming along with the rest of the crowd. Right up front, next to the stage, was the campaign staff led by Ken Mehlman; Matthew Dowd, the campaign's chief strategist; and Tom Josefiak, the campaign's general counsel. And right next to them were members of my family, including my uncle, Mark Vincent, who'd come with his wife, Linda, from Casper, Wyoming, and my aunt Sue, who had flown in from Idaho.

I have to admit that I had mixed feelings while I was up there waving at the crowd. I was so happy and excited that we'd won, that eighteen months of hard work had paid off, and that Dad and President Bush had been re-elected, but I was also sad that the campaign was over. It had been physically and emotionally exhausting, but it had also been one of the most rewarding experiences of my life. I knew that I was going to miss going to campaign headquarters every morning or getting on the plane and flying to the next event. I also knew it was the end of Dad's last campaign and, therefore, the end of my last one, too. . . .

I greatly admire the skills and abilities of professional campaign consultants—experts who spend their lives working on a series of campaigns for many different candidates—but I've never seen it as a career for myself. I ran Vice Presidential Operations for the Bush-Cheney campaign because I love and believe so strongly in my father as a candidate, as a person, and as a leader. I can't imagine working for anyone else, and since Dad's made it very clear that he won't be running for office again, the 2004 presidential race was my last campaign as well.

Unless, of course, someone talks Dad into heading up another search committee.

About the Author

MARY CHENEY served as the personal aide to her father, the vice presidential nominee, during the 2000 presidential campaign. In 2004, she was director of vice presidential operations for Bush-Cheney '04. Ms. Cheney is a graduate of Colorado College and holds an M.B.A. from the University of Denver. She currently works for AOL, Inc., and lives in Great Falls, Virginia, with her partner, Heather Poe.

Printed in the United States
By Bookmasters